Table of Contents

Grad's Guide to
GRADUATE ADMISSIONS ESSAYS

Colleen Reding

PRUFROCK PRESS INC.
WACO, TEXAS

Library of Congress Cataloging-in-Publication Data

Reding, Colleen, 1987-
  Grad's guide to graduate admissions essays : examples from real students who got into top schools
/ by Colleen Reding.
     pages cm
  ISBN 978-1-61821-393-8 (pbk.)
  1. College applications--United States. 2.   Universities and colleges--United States--Graduate
work--Admission. 3. Exposition (Rhetoric) 4. Essay--Authorship. I. Title.
  LB2351.52.U6R44 2015
  378.1'6160973--dc23
                              2015001961

Edited by Lacy Compton

Cover and layout design by Raquel Trevino

ISBN-13: 978-1-61821-393-8

At the time of this book's publication, all facts and figures cited are the most current available; all
telephone numbers, addresses, and website URLs are accurate and active; all publications, organizations, websites, and other resources exist as described in this book; and all have been verified. The
authors and Prufrock Press make no warranty or guarantee concerning the information and materials
given out by organizations or content found at websites, and we are not responsible for any changes
that occur after this book's publication. If you find an error or believe that a resource listed here is
not as described, please contact Prufrock Press.

Prufrock Press Inc.
P.O. Box 8813
Waco, TX 76714-8813
Phone: (800) 998-2208
Fax: (800) 240-0333
http://www.prufrock.com

Grad's Guide to

GRADUATE
ADMISSIONS
ESSAYS

NOTES

The contents of this book represent the original works of the essays' respective authors. Any attempt to copy from this written work or other sources would be considered plagiarism.

Some identifying information such as the names of employers, professors, and family members has been modified or extracted at the discretion of the essays' contributors. Additionally, minor changes were applied to some essays for editorial and style purposes.

INTRODUCTION

Mastering the Admissions Essay

Grad's Guide to Graduate Admissions Essays provides more than 50 successful admissions essays straight from the source—recent Georgetown University graduates making the transition to earning advanced degrees at highly selective graduate programs. Harvard, Yale, Columbia, Duke, Stanford, Cornell, and Northwestern are just a few of the universities to which these students were admitted. The goal of the guide is to provide reassurance that you don't have to write your essay about the successful tech start-up you founded or groundbreaking research publication you drafted in order to be accepted at some of the world's most competitive and prestigious programs.

At the same time, that essay you wrote for undergraduate admissions about your high school basketball team's triumph at regionals isn't going to cut it anymore. Highlighting experiences that give insight into your personality, your life experiences, and your commitment to furthering your education is the key to any successful statement. Admissions officers want to see leadership skills, a passion for the chosen field of study, and sincerity in the writing. In addition to conveying these qualities, it is important to also ensure that your essay is well-written, as this essay serves as a writing sample for the admissions committee. This guidebook gives a multitude of examples of successful essays in terms of content as well as format and provides tips ranging from how to brainstorm effectively to how to structure the essay. Crafting a strong essay is no easy task, and it may be difficult to determine where to begin, but you've come to the right place.

While utilizing *Grad's Guide to Graduate Admission Essays* as you begin drafting your own essay, be sure to read all essays, not just the ones matching your own desired degree. Whether applying to medical school or to a Ph.D. program in anthropology, the same key elements remain essential to creating effective admissions essays. Additionally, when reading the essays, it is important to keep in mind that the essay is not the only factor that plays into admissions decisions. The authors of these essays were admitted to their programs of choice for a variety of reasons, including test scores, academic achievements, professional experience, and other admissions criteria. The essays are provided as a means for you to begin thinking about what works and where to start, while receiving valuable advice from the essays' authors.

In business school, you learn through case studies, in law school you learn from previous court decisions, and within the humanities field, you will be drawing on the teachings of scholars. No matter which graduate program or profession you select, learning by example will inevitably be a critical piece of your academic endeavors. Because of that, this guidebook is not structured by a series of lessons on personal statements followed by some samples. Instead, let the successful admissions essays included in this work be your guide. Not only will the following essays assist you with providing insight into best practices, but the authors have also included their own pieces of advice for navigating through the admissions process. From determining how to explain a career shift within your essay to making the decision to return to school in the first place, every graduate school decision you may be facing has been tackled before. Why not take advice from those who have survived the application process and successfully gained admission to the schools of their choice?

Within this guidebook, you will review essays that fall within the category of personal statements, statements of purpose, and those that respond to specific prompts. It is essential that you follow the guidelines of the particular programs to which you are applying to ensure that you are providing the universities with the information that they are seeking. Personal statements tend to offer the most freedom to choose a topic that allows readers to learn something new about you that might not be found elsewhere in the application. Statements of purpose should include details that expand on what you plan to pursue academically and what led you to the determination that graduate study is the next step for you. Finally, when writing within a specific prompt, ensure that you are answering all parts of the question, but remember to think creatively and also use the opportunity to demonstrate your writing skills.

I hope that you enjoy getting to know the authors within this work through their successful essays as much as I have. I am confident that their journeys will resonate with your own graduate school ambitions—rest assured that you are not alone and that you too can achieve your goals in higher education.

PART

I

LAW

CHAPTER

1

University of Houston Law Center

Each successive door required a unique key. Buzzers sounded, signifying that the previous door was secured and the next could be opened. Two guarded driveways, one metal detector, and seven locking doors later, I was standing in Ward 10 on the top floor of a criminal mental hospital in the roughest area of Washington, DC. In what is certainly an intentional metaphor, the maximum-security patients are housed on the highest floor—a constant reminder of the distance to the doors to freedom. The words of the hospital psychologist were still ringing in my ears. "Never let a patient stand behind you," he warned, "And always wear closed-toed shoes because you could pick up a disease off the floor that you might never get rid of." With those intimidating words and a healthy dose of curiosity and adventure, I began my 4-year relationship with the men of St. Elizabeth's Hospital.

In my experience, the only way to discover my true capacity is to step outside my comfort zone. With 4 years' worth of Friday afternoons spent playing board games alongside, writing poetry with, and generally just listening to men who have pled "not guilty by reason of insanity," I learned that my will to serve others is stronger than fear and stereotype as I have put a face—many faces—to the term "mental illness." These men were diagnosed with schizophrenia, bipolar disorder, and sexual psychopathy, and committed crimes including rape and murder. Unlike a civil mental hospital where patients might only stay 2 weeks, most patients in this maximum-security forensic mental hospital stay upwards of 30 years, which allowed me to develop a rapport with certain patients over my college career. If the patients had family who visited when they were first institutionalized, they had long ago stopped coming, and we were generally the only visitors any patient received all week.

I understood when a student joined our club one week but was scared off and never returned. I do not claim that this is the Friday afternoon activity for everyone, but I found my niche in St. Elizabeth's and I am glad the psychologist's warnings did not scare me off that first day. By my fourth year, the patients saw me as more than someone with whom to play Jenga, but as someone with whom they could confide. Some patients wanted to tell me about their crimes. Others spoke of their rediscovered faith and wanted to discuss Bible and Koran passages about repentance and forgiveness. One amazed me with his knowledge of the philosophies of Plato and Locke. Another studied the dictionary all week long in preparation for our weekly game of Scrabble and took great pride in beating all of the Georgetown students. Still there were

WRITER'S WORDS OF WISDOM

You don't have to have some out-of-this-world, once-in-a-lifetime experience to write a good essay. You can start with the seed of a small personal anecdote that doesn't seem to have any Earth-shattering significance and then grow it into a universal theme that is important to you or show how that anecdote is representative of you as a whole. Additionally, unless the prompt specifically asks, my gut feeling is to avoid the "why I want to be a lawyer" or the "I've wanted to be a lawyer since I was a kid" essay because admissions will read 10,000 of those. They know you want to be a lawyer—that's why you applied. Tell them something about you as a person.

others who did not interact with us at all except to stand and receive us with a handshake as we entered and exited.

Above all else, reflection on my time at St. Elizabeth's is a constant reminder of the tangible influence one person can exert on another's life. A patient once told me I was "the best part of his week," and I will never forget that. While I did not have the power to release patients from the mental hospital, petition to have their sentences reduced, or quiet the voices in their heads, I did have the power to commit to being there every Friday with a positive attitude and an open mind.

I do not claim that writing poetry with these men relates to law school or that it can speak to the kind of lawyer I will be, but this experience has forever changed what kind of person I am. Watching one man tenderly hold a picture of a 2-year-old little girl—his daughter—whom he hadn't seen in more than 15 years, I became more attuned to the loneliness of others. After hearing their stories of mental illness triggered by drug use, childhood abuse, and war, I became slower to judge and quicker to listen. When certain members of the staff suggested that we cease all physical contact with the patients, I became painfully aware of the inherent human need for the dignity that comes from a respectful hand-shake. I looked forward to most Fridays, but knowing how much they eagerly awaited our visits pushed me to make the trip on icy cold days or afternoons when I felt overwhelmed with schoolwork and, in the process, I noticed myself getting better at following through on all of my commitments. In 4 years, I witnessed verbal and physical altercations between patients, I was evacuated after a cryptic coded announcement, I saw the instability and felt the anxiety in the new arrivals, and I celebrated with those who were being moved down to medium security, only to watch them return to maximum security a few weeks later. In seeing the rawness and vulnerability of mental illness and incarceration in the men of St. Elizabeth's, I became more aware of my own humanity.

> **REALIZING CHARACTER COUNTS**
>
> In the author's account of this particular aspect of her life, readers not only learn about the author's interest in volunteering but also discover the author's other qualities of being humble and authentic without the author coming out and stating it.

CHAPTER 2

Fordham University School of Law

"Attention on the concourse: Continental Airlines flight 1285 to Washington, DC will be delayed an additional hour due to technical difficulties. We thank you for your patience." I found myself sitting in the Houston airport, waiting for the flight back to DC that now signaled the end of my workweek. The delay meant missing a friend's birthday party and spending my Friday night alone in an airport. Working as a paralegal in the Department of Justice hadn't exactly turned out the way I had anticipated.

This wasn't the first time that I had questioned my decision to leave my former job managing a cupcake shop. At that moment, I would have traded anything to worry about whether or not we had enough chocolate cupcakes to make it until closing instead of lying awake and wondering if I had made enough copies of our exhibits to publish to the jury the next day. It had been difficult leaving an exciting job at a rapidly expanding business where I managed more than 50 employees. But here was an opportunity to work in a field that I had become passionate about, having been exposed to both the judicial and the legislative sides of the law in several internship roles during my undergraduate years, at both the federal and state levels.

STAYING HUMBLE

The author conveys the ability to overcome difficult circumstances without bragging or coming across as overly confident.

Traveling each week was but one of the unforeseen challenges my new role would bring. My team was understaffed and underresourced and it quickly became apparent that I would not receive any training. I took it upon myself to learn the ropes, determined to excel quickly.

After working for 6 weeks, I prepared my attorney coworkers for a 3-week trial with nine defendants. In addition to being away from home every week, having the weight of a federal trial on your shoulders was, to say the least, a bit overwhelming. However, I found that my organizational skills and ability to assess any issues or obstacles that arose in a logical and timely manner were essential to achieve what seemed to be an impossible goal. I learned quickly to adapt to last minute changes and to pay attention to the details, no matter how seemingly insignificant.

Despite the incredible stress inherent in working on a federal trial for the first time, the experience of sitting at the counsel table and watching the prosecutors firsthand was inspiring. My respect for our justice system, which at times still frustrates and disappoints even the truest of believers, grew tremendously, as did as my respect for the attorneys I worked with night and day to ensure we presented our case in a manner worthy of the federal courtroom where we spent each day. I gained an enormous appreciation for the gravity of our work and its potential for impact on society as a whole.

Through many late nights in the courthouse, my motivation never faltered. In retrospect, I believe that the isolation of living in a strange place for five nights each week, and yes, even the anxiety of the entire experience, was perhaps the best thing that could have happened to help my concentration as I was transitioning into a new job that involved matters of such enormous consequence. After the guilty verdicts were read, and our chief litigator wrote to DC claiming that my drive to succeed was an indispensable part of the end result, my exhaustion was replaced by exhilaration and a profound motivation to do it again.

As I prepared myself to board my flight back to DC that Friday night, I considered all of the events that I had missed back home and the friends and family members that I hadn't seen in months. Despite the sacrifices I'd made, I knew there was no going back from this invaluable experience. I had found a challenging and unique position that kept me driven each day and inspired me to work harder. As I boarded the plane, I knew that I would be on the flight back to Houston on Monday morning, eager to begin work on our next trial.

WRITER'S WORDS OF WISDOM

Before you apply to law school, make sure that practicing law is something that you are passionate and excited about. Spend some time working in or observing others in the legal field. If so, trust your instincts and stay driven.

CHAPTER
3

University of Chicago Law School

For a split second, the rat and I locked eyes. The critter casually continued gnawing at a crumb from my dinner before disappearing into my host Cindy's bedroom. I was indifferent and continued playing paper, rock, scissors with Cindy's three kids. Cindy was one of the women I worked with closely on the women's empowerment program I was interning for an international NGO in Malawi. She was a hefty-sized, incredibly jolly woman who commanded respect from whomever she met. About halfway through my time in Malawi, after my fondness for children had become painfully obvious, she invited me to her home so that I could play with her own kids.

That's when I found out that she was a widow. Guiltily, I realized I was not even surprised. In a country where one out of every 10 people is HIV positive, the devastating effects of one of recent history's most destructive and ruthless endemics somehow haunted practically everyone I had met. Everyone has a story. One more tragic than the next.

> **WRITER'S WORDS OF WISDOM**
>
> If your grad program allows you to defer enrollment, seriously consider doing it. Deferrals give you an opportunity to do things you might not be able to do after grad school with the security of a spot at a grad program waiting for you. There's no rush to start school right after undergrad in the grand scheme of things.

Strangely, I left Malawi not crippled with despair and grief, although I certainly fought such emotions throughout my stay, but filled with hope and inspired by the strength of the people of Malawi. I desperately wanted to return to Malawi; little did I know how soon that day would come.

While I was in Malawi that first summer, I became friendly with some of the teenagers who lived in the neighborhood I was staying in. At first, they were only eager to ask me if I had ever met Jennifer Lopez or Madonna, but they eventually began to share their personal lives with me. Most had lost a family member to AIDS. Many lived in poverty. Yet, they spent the most time recounting familiar teenage problems with their peers: gossip, boyfriend/girlfriend issues, jealousy, and petty theft. It dawned on me that these kids were facing the same growing pains every teenager experiences. When I asked them how they dealt with these issues, they said the teachers would usually punish them, occasionally beating or whipping them. Although I was disappointed with how these conflicts were handled, I understood that the teachers were overworked, underpaid, and understaffed and probably did not possess the time or resources to handle student conflicts in a more effective manner.

MAKING IT PERSONAL

Good essays will utilize an example of a meaningful experience to pinpoint interest in a given field. Great essays will go a step beyond and show how the author internalized the experience. Here, the author offers insight into why Malawi was so significant and how it continues to impact the author's life after Africa.

When I was back in the United States, I began thinking about my experiences as a peer mediator when I was in middle school. A group of students and I had been trained by a professional mediator in conflict resolution, listening, and communication skills in order to serve as peer mediators and assist fellow students in devising their own solutions to conflicts. My peers could come up with their own solutions, their own contracts, and their own laws to govern their relationships. Could this model be applied to Malawi? Initially, I was apprehensive. Who was I to go into an African country and impose a program that has only been tested in the West? Yet, the idea kept nagging at me. As someone who hopes to work toward advancing social justice in the world, I greatly value empowerment as a tool for change. Peer mediation is a fundamentally empowering concept for all involved, in that it provides students with agency over their own lives and trusts them to resolve their own issues without the intervention of an authority figure. Malawian students could be involved in something they could be proud of, something they could call their own, and something that would tangibly improve their direct community. When I saw the opportunity to apply for funding through a special grant, I went for it, pledging to myself that I would make every effort to make sure the project was contextually and culturally catered.

When the funding came through, I contacted every conflict resolution center and expert I could find and madly searched for a curriculum that had been successfully implemented in Africa. Although I found no such curriculum, I amassed valuable advice before heading back to Malawi. I worked with the NGO staff to change the role-plays and examples to situations familiar to local life. The staff and I identified two community schools that we thought would benefit from the program. The director of one of the schools was incredibly receptive. He explained to me that his teachers were tired of disciplining their students and that his students needed more leadership opportunities.

As I stood in front of the students on the first day of training, I felt uncomfortable. Here I was, a White girl from America about to "teach" students only a few years younger than myself a foreign concept they could hardly pronounce at that point. Yet, I realized that if I allowed my discomfort to become visible, it would only serve as an additional barrier between the students and me. I dove right into the training's interactive questions and activities. The kids amazed me. They absorbed every concept I presented them and asked me challenging questions that proved they were already thinking about the application of the skills they were learning. They performed role-plays with gusto, excitedly devising their own potential conflicts to resolve. My initial discomfort

SHOWING INITIATIVE

The author does an excellent job of identifying a problem and detailing her proactive approach to tackling the implementation of her program.

dissolved as I found myself increasingly invested in the lives of my students. The highlight of the trainings for me was the day when I did not have to say a single word during an exercise not because it was executed flawlessly, but because the other students were doing the critique completely on their own. They had taken ownership of the program. They no longer needed me, and that was the best feeling in the world.

CHAPTER 4

University of Florida Levin College of Law

It was at the age of 13 that I was finally allowed to accompany my mother to work. I had difficulty containing my excitement in the days leading up to that morning when we finally left together to embark on our journey. This was it, I remember thinking, my rite of passage.

Driving up to the ominous looking building where I was to spend my day, my feeling of triumph proved ephemeral, as apprehension took its place. I hesitantly followed through what seemed to be a never-ending series of hallways and security codes, until I was informed that we had arrived. As my mother held the door open for me, I crossed the threshold that would open my eyes to a new reality—one that would have an impact on the rest of my life.

I was surprised that the first person I saw, as I looked around, was a girl my own age. She had several bruises and her eye was swollen shut, and I immediately understood that she was a victim of domestic violence. This realization that someone my own age had been physically abused overwhelmed me with a shock I had never experienced. I must have been led away from the scene, but my body felt paralyzed and I did not realize I was moving. The image of the wound on the girl's face preoccupied all my other thoughts.

My mother worked at a shelter that protected women and families from domestic abuse. Her primary role was providing legal counseling to the families who had been subjected to domestic assault, drafting orders of protection against their perpetrators and defending them in court. In her spare time, she volunteered at the shelter and raised funds that were necessary to sustain it as a nonprofit organization.

"Are you feeling alright?" my mother asked. With these words, my epiphany was brought to a halt with a lacerating force. I was now standing in a new room with new people, all of whom had looks of concern on their faces as they stared down at me. I had been too consumed by my thoughts to realize that I had even moved. Now finding it hard to articulate words, let alone answer the question, silence permeated the room as everyone waited for my response. My mother asked again if I was OK, and if I still wanted to help.

I wanted to help more than ever. Face to face with the horrors of domestic abuse, I wanted to do all that was in my power to make a difference. I began regularly volunteering at the shelter, a decision that exposed me to not only the tragedies of domestic abuse, but also how the shelter was able to help so many people. It was when I entered high school that I was given the opportunity to expand my personal commitment to help. Using the resources at my school, I started a student interest group and organized fundraisers to support and raise awareness for domestic abuse. It gave me a sense of accomplishment that I was able to help the shelter and inspire others to do the same.

My life took a drastic turn when my mother suddenly became sick and passed away when I was 17. In the wake of the tragedy, I was able to find a silver lining, although it was difficult to do so at first. The experience made me a stronger person and forced me to reconsider much

> **WRITER'S WORDS OF WISDOM**
>
> I would sit down and really think about the reason why you want to go to graduate school in the first place. From there, I would write out a list of those reasons. When you sit down to write, make sure that you are emphasizing those points. It can also help in developing a theme for your paper when you look at all those reasons collectively, or help you to figure out the stronger or more compelling ideas.

that I had previously taken for granted. My mother had been my role model, but even so, I had never truly recognized the extent of what she had accomplished both in her professional and personal life until she was gone. She had touched others' lives, including my own, and she had done so through her work, benevolence, and commitment. Honing her practice of law to protect women and children who were victims of domestic abuse, my mother had not only salvaged the low-funded organization to provide a comfortable refuge for the families, but also defended their rights and safety through her legal advocacy. Although I had known all along that I respected her work, I now realized that I wanted to follow in her footsteps and continue her legacy.

I like to think that I have begun to do so. My experiences working at the shelter first introduced me to the importance of social work and generated an interest that would stay with me for the rest of my life. When I entered Georgetown, I began working at the university's Center for Social Justice in order to further this interest, an experience that has provided me various opportunities to become involved in not-for-profit programs—from tutoring in low-income public schools in the District of Columbia to serving on a student panel that promotes philanthropy and tolerance. I hope through doing social work I am having a meaningful impact on others' lives, just as my role model had done her whole life. I have learned that life is simply too short and too fleeting to do otherwise. With this perspective, I have expanded my horizons, a development that has allowed me to be appreciative of how fortunate I have been, and with that, how important it is to help others who are not as fortunate.

PROVIDING EFFECTIVE TRANSITIONS

Here, the author successfully transitions from discussing her inspiration to what she has done to put her interests into action. It shows commitment to the line of work and self-motivation.

With my graduation rapidly approaching, I see law school as the next step on my horizon. My interest in law is due to my exposure to what legal advocacy can accomplish. I hope to one day become a public interest lawyer, providing legal services to public or government agencies.

I know that I will always have an interest in social work, and specifically fighting against domestic violence, and so I hope that with a law degree I will be given that much greater of an opportunity to make a difference and address the multitude of injustices that exist in our society.

CHAPTER
5

Emory University School of Law

A 3-foot box of lacquered pine doesn't leave much room to mentally or physically stretch, suffocating even with the amusements of half-witted graffiti from some past steward. Gearing up for college I was a dreamer. Back on the task of an admissions statement now, it reminds me of scrawling a 500-worded ode to cosmic servitude as an aspiring folkster, comparing a high school mission trip to Dylan's "A-Hard Rain's A-Gonna Fall," stanza by stanza, in retrospectively endearing naiveté. Which is why early forays into development economics came as such a soul-gripping surprise then, when poring over some of the world's most far-reaching and humbling questions was done in a cubicle under an isolated florescent glow, tracing inscrutable equations with clean gnawed fingers. Even as a self-aware introvert, this claustrophobia was something wholly new and unsettling.

Midway through my sophomore year I started working in the library's student-owned coffee shop—a meager, income-induced pursuit that led to a profound ideological shift I never saw coming. A steady stream of like-riddled aspiring Earth-shakers trickled single file through a pamphlet-strewn jamb, on the scent of caffeine. For a minute and a half each, I commanded a stage—a chance to prod, tell a quick joke, trade thoughts from a recent lecture. Behind that counter, I found the power to kick down unintentional barricades on both sides that higher education is wont to create and came to understand the overlooked potential encased anywhere footsteps cross.

By my senior year, I was working at a well-loved bar near campus, waiting tables between other obligations. I got to see eyes red and dry with aimless conviction from term papers one day, scanning between espresso options with wary taps to appraise the vitals, that then turned moist and blue an evening later over a pitcher of wild conversation. Most weeks I spent 30–40 hours between the two hubs, increasingly animated with the confidence that there was something so captivating about the work beyond its simple surface. There is a therapeutic quality to that engagement I don't know how I could have found otherwise. It's an art form of at-a-glance empathy—knowing when to lock ears, console, vent, beam warmly, compliment generously, ask the right questions, or recall personal details—in whatever display, mutually assuring that a human connection is never as distant as it can seem.

WRITER'S WORDS OF WISDOM

Go visit, and do it right. I had repeated existential crises crawling through prospective student portals, thinking I may just be destined instead to plod out my days in an anonymous assembly line instead of all this. The reason for visiting is twofold.

Like trying to keep track of the cast of characters in a silent movie, it's not an easy job for the admissions staff to keep a hard drive of applicant files from getting shuffled. Making your way to a chair in their office by hell or high water, asking the right questions and showing genuine interest achieves so much more than saying, "I'm a big fan of your program, Dean" in the essays. You get the chance to humanize yourself with a terrible story about running out of gas while lost in Detroit or an explanation

continues on page 21

It made me a realist, too. The callowness of a wide-eyed gaze at a blue-green world was slowly replaced by an understanding of the infinitely important interactions and actions of every day. In a fantastic performance by Elvis Costello in the White House, playing "Penny Lane" with President Obama in his audience, he opens saying, "Music is often an 'us against them' proposition. And the next song you're going to hear is named after a place from which my mother comes from about half a mile away so you can imagine when this thing of wonder and beauty came on the radio, myself as a young boy, my dad, my mom, and the cat all stopped and took notice." For me, my experiences working in that environment and giving weight to each personal moment rinsed the paralyzing confines of "us and them" or "mine and theirs" from my mind, allowing me to redraw the battle lines to allow for collaboration. I could illuminate my own studies next to the radiant brilliance of my peers rather than fumble with a match alone in the dark, and strive to provide the same enlightenment for them. Even with countless nights left to race dawn against deadlines in a fortified corner of the library, it ceased to be a lonely endeavor once the lives and work of those around me became more and more enmeshed with my own, sharing the same slew of guideposts and lettered awnings to keep pushing forward down the lane.

What has thrilled me about pursuing a law degree focused on environmental and resource issues is its simultaneous breadth and concision. I know the field is and will increasingly be

continued from page 20

of the screeching jazz accidentally leaking from the headphones tucked in your jacket. And it gives you the chance to follow up with the admissions staff with more questions or simple thank-you notes later on down the line, which in the world of applications is like wishing for more wishes.

Second, what you are jumping into is the rare opportunity to open a map and throw darts. The change of scenery could be just as important as the program you're gunning for, so don't ignore its importance until your lease for a lifeless suburban basement is already signed. Go alone, fake like you belong there, be sure there is a go-to spot for tea and good lighting between classes, make your way through the surrounding neighborhood, locate welcoming faces, and get behind the scenes to be sure it all comes as advertised.

charged with attacking among the most complex regulatory issues and far-reaching problems we face this century and beyond, many with stunningly elegant economic and technological solutions that are slowed by political stalemate and uncertainty. The stakes could not be higher, with huge markets to make, break, or maintain a stake. At the same time, there is a unique and invaluable potential for localized impacts, as households, neighborhoods, cities, and on up the line become laboratories for the advancement of new policies. My experiences have taught me so far to cultivate big ideas through small, engaged efforts. Even when the starched white apron comes off and the lingering bite of fresh grounds is finally lifted from my favorite shirts, I'll hold that dearly, in my ears and in my eyes.

CHAPTER

6

Georgetown University Law Center

I am unabashedly a girly girl and have embraced this characteristic since childhood; by refusing to wear anything but dresses and "princess clothes" for far too long, it seemed that I would turn into a stereotypical real little princess. Yet not every young girl would juxtapose a viewing of her *Grease* VHS with the *Indiana Jones* trilogy, nor would every little princess jump back and forth between aspirations of being a prima ballerina and an FBI agent within the blink of a twinkling little eye. I have grown into a young woman who is still admittedly a girly girl, but who breaks from convention by always adding a twist. This is one particular facet of my personality that I am especially proud of—less sugar and more spice with everything nice.

One prominent example of this "personal twist" has been in my choice of a major in Classics at Georgetown—or rather my passion for Latin. I couldn't begin to name the multitude of my female friends who love writing and language as well, though predominantly due to its power to evoke emotion. My own love of language is something undeniably different. Instead of joining the ranks of English majors lining up around me, I was (and continue to be) captivated by Classics. While the heroes of Ancient Rome are oftentimes lauded for their military prestige, I am in awe of the understanding of the power of words alone that Latin authors beautifully demonstrate: not only their ability to move emotionally, but also to persuade masterfully, and most interestingly to uphold account-ability and responsibility successfully within society. What better intro-duction to these capacities of well-crafted language can be found than: a winning legal oration by Cicero, a study of morality and handbook marketed as a "biography" by Suetonius, or a list of bragging rights dis-seminated as personal propaganda by the Emperor Augustus.

Undoubtedly due to my girly girl exterior, I have withstood count-less skeptical looks and exclamations of disbelief when identifying myself as a Classics major (or even stomached snide retorts of "I thought my father was like the only person who studied that, and he's a big geek"). Subsequently, I have come to sadly suspect that I am a member of a rare breed as an outgoing young lady who loves studying a dead language; I may insist upon fre-quently updating my brightly colored nails and still wearing dresses almost daily, but that doesn't hinder my ability to produce a mean translation of Virgil's *Aeneid*.

STANDING OUT FROM THE STACK

This is the kind of essay that makes admissions officers think, "I have to meet this girl." The essay combines the perfect amount of confidence and self-deprecating humor, allowing the author's personality to shine through each paragraph.

This love of articulation even prompted me to study abroad in Dublin for all of last year in an attempt to gain some of the famed gift of gab for myself, instead of following my fellow Classics majors to semester programs in Italy and Greece (though I selected a school with a strong Classics program, a perfect fit for all of my interests).

In light of my fascination with the power of words, I hope to add yet a new twist into my life. As a perpetual performer during my childhood and adolescence, one would assume that I would be drawn directly to the stage of the courtroom and the high-profile role of a litigator; how-ever, due to the amazing opportunities for summer internships that have come my way, my eyes have been opened to the limitless potential that the law provides in terms of working with words. During my time in music licensing at a record label in Manhattan, I was drawn to the dance of drafting an air-tight contract that coincides with both parties' interests. Even further, my summer in DC as the Legislative Director of an up-and-coming nonprofit plunged me happily into the world of drafting language for bills and resolutions in both the House and Senate. In my future endeavors, I hope that my little personal twists continue to open new doors and add a little spice to my life, while my love of articulation and language consistently provides a guiding force.

WRITER'S WORDS OF WISDOM

Embrace your sense of humor. Instead of manufacturing an emotional story, making someone laugh or smile can be just as effective (and persuasive).

CHAPTER
7

Boston College Law School

"We just want to be together during this hard time. She has cancer and she won't make it much longer. Is there anything we can do?" As the client told me her story and I prepared an application for travel documents that would allow her sibling to enter the United States, I began to understand what this visit would mean to them. Despite the geographic distance their respective citizenships implied, these three sisters had maintained their close relationship over the years, and when one of them had been diagnosed with aggressive, stage IV endometrial cancer with a prognosis of less than 2 months, they prayed for the opportunity to be together one last time. When I received notice that the U.S. consulate in Mexico had approved the application, I understood the extent to which immigration law has the potential to transform the lives of its clients.

I also witnessed an attorney's ability to protect not only familial bonds but also cultural ties through language. Both my personal and work experiences have demonstrated the profound

TELLING A STORY

The author utilizes the very effective technique of telling a story of a specific work-related project to convey her experience, interests, and desire for further education. Through her storytelling, her excitement for the field of work becomes readily apparent.

cultural power of language and its effect on a community. With the unrelenting dream of hearing his grandchildren speak his native language, my grandfather adamantly refused to speak to me in English despite his fluency in both languages. Sadly, it was not until after his death that I began to feel his passion for my estranged culture.

With a Cuban mother and a Mexican father, hearing Spanish was a part of my life, but never being forced to speak it distanced me from a part of my own heritage. Immersed in a culture similar to my own, my study abroad experiences in Argentina demonstrated the cultural significance of a shared language and linguistically reconnected me to my grandfather's passion for his cultural ties. Though the peculiar combination of my mother's rushed Cuban phrases, my father's Mexican clarity, and my unique Argentine accent resembles little of the past my grandfather treasured, the reality of our common language unites our experiences.

PUTTING THE PIECES TOGETHER

Family, work experience, culture, language, and law are all essential components of this essay; the author effectively weaves these themes together to explain how they all play a role in the applicant's determination to apply to law school. The author maintains a strong balance while combining these ideas.

I can only begin to imagine the difficulties my grandparents faced when they emigrated from Cuba and Mexico, building a life from scratch while trying to maintain a connection to their culture and language. Constantly moving from one relative's house to another, unsure of where they would end up, my grandparents never had anyone to provide any hope of stability or constancy. I want to be an immediate reminder to immigrant families that they do not have to relinquish their culture even though they are far from home.

The most conspicuous and lasting reminder of a culture is a language that provides a stable connection to a home country. By providing a sense of constancy, language plays a formative role in the establishment of a new home. Through a law degree and a career as an immigration attorney, I want to reach out to immigrant families, Hispanic families in particular, by establishing an immediate connection through a common language. I want to be a constant for families experiencing displacement due to their homeland's inability to offer stability and security.

For immigrants, language can also serve as a divisive force and result in isolation. Rather than perpetuating their existence at the margins of society, these families should be integrated into our system that already heavily relies on their presence as workers. By emphasizing the strong linguistic and cultural continuities that exist between homeland communities and those in the United States, these new Americans can promote greater social incorporation rather than segregation.

By giving my time to these immigrant families, I can relate my personal experience of reconnecting to my own heritage. By taking full advantage of the opportunity to attend law school and applying the knowledge while reaching out to immigrant families, I hope to establish community through a common language that can help create a new home and maintain strong ties to unique cultures.

WRITER'S WORDS OF WISDOM

When I started applying to law school, I kept getting hung up on planning out what I was going to say in my personal statement but never actually getting anything on paper. The best advice I could give is to just start writing. Sit down, and write something. Odds are you won't use 90% of what you write the first time, but it will get you started and leave you with something concrete to work with and bounce off of other people.

CHAPTER
8

George Mason University School of Law

There are two ways to play the flute. In solitude, the flutist is in full control of the composition. Each sound produced by the instrument is distinct. Slight variations dramatically alter a given composition, so that one has to articulate each phrase with extreme care. With others, the flute morphs into a vehicle of companionship. Blending with the group, the flutist injects passion and enthusiasm into the music without overwhelming the sound of the entire band.

I nervously held my newly purchased flute in my hand. The instrument shone. My high school flute instructor stood over me as I began to play the assigned piece. Although I stumbled over some of the notes, I felt content with my progress and expected only approbation from my teacher. Instead, my instructor had other plans.

"Rest your flute and close your eyes," she instructed. "Listen closely to the recording."

As soon as I shut my eyes, the orchestra's harmonious notes blended together to form a mosaic of sounds. I could see the conductor swirling his delicate wrist to the ebb and flow of the orchestra's graceful rhythm. I listened for the flute section's melodic entrance. As the other instruments danced around the melody with fanciful trills, the flutes stretched each phrase, pushing the boundaries while keeping in time. Although far from an experienced musician, I heard the discrepancy between my reading of the piece and the orchestra's interpretation. Instead of playing merely what was written on the page, the orchestra personalized the composition by manipulating rhythms, varying the tempo, and altering the dynamics. I returned to the assigned piece. The black notes contrasted starkly with the white paper. I stared at the composition, attempting to create a coherent story out of the various notes. Slowly, I began to realize that music is far from "black and white." Each piece can be played in a slightly different, yet noticeably distinct, manner.

The crowd erupted into applause as the Georgetown basketball team sprinted onto the court. I drew my flute to my lips, anticipating the downbeat of the Georgetown fight song. As soon as the sound of the trumpets roared into the arena, the rest of the pep band joined in the melody. My fingers ran smoothly over the slightly tarnished keys while I moved in tandem with the flute section to the beat of the base drum. Each carefully planned movement created flashes of color as the band dipped and swayed in the stands. Georgetown fans stood as a sea of blue and gray, taunting the rival team. I articulated each note with extreme care so as to remain in harmony with the other flutists. The band's sound depended on the restraint and concentration of each member. The excitement felt by each band member enhanced the overall enthusiasm of the group, pushing the volume to an overwhelming level.

ABIDING BY "LESS IS MORE"

The author incorporates one carefully considered theme, creating a beautifully crafted and straightforward statement.

There are two ways I play the flute. Alone, I seek to find my own musical voice while with others, I exercise restraint. I hope to expand upon these traits long after I put my flute to rest. Although always aware of established rules and order, I will continue to explore the way in which society is shaped by those who have the determination and foresight to create their own melody.

CHAPTER

9

University of Texas School of Law

As I forced on my third layer of clothing and stepped outside my front door that brisk January morning, the thermostat read 19 degrees Fahrenheit. Bundled in warm hats, woven scarves, and thick gloves, my five roommates and I began our march down Pennsylvania Avenue toward the Capitol, but the crowds before us soon halted our journey. Millions of people and an expanse of frozen grass made the sizable distance from the inauguration platform seem like miles. Feeling as though I'd soon be crushed and swallowed by the growing crowd, I began to wonder, why does my being here really matter to me?

While waiting, my mind leapt back to 6 months earlier when I had last looked out a large third-floor window of the Chief Deputy Whip's office in the Capitol Building, gazing down across the long, green panel of grass where I now stood among millions. If I had been peering out the window now, maybe I would not see green grass at all, but instead a blue and brown quilt-like pattern of the tops of hats and full heads of hair woven tightly together. I could still remember most of the photographs, posters, and framed newspaper clippings that decorated Representative Lewis's oak office walls. The most vivid was a black and white photograph of the Big Six: Mr. Lewis alongside the five other most powerful leaders of the American Civil Rights Movement. Also memorable was a framed image of 23-year-old Lewis delivering a keynote speech at the March on Washington in August 1963.

Without warning, the suffocating mass surrounding me roared upon first sight of the President on the Jumbrotrons that lined the lawn. Still waiting for the speech to begin, my mind throbbed with the unanswered question: Why does my presence here matter?

DRAFTING LAW SCHOOL PERSONAL STATEMENTS

There are few rules, so with the freedom to write what you like, be sure to write well and present yourself positively. The author picks a meaningful experience and reveals a strong ability to question and to reflect.

During the 20-minute inaugural address, the screens never wavered from the President. Yet, as he neared the end of his remarks, he took a deep breath, and explained that America's liberty is the reason why he, "a man whose father less than 60 years ago might not have been served at a local restaurant, can now stand before you to take a most sacred oath." And in a very rare moment, the camera's focus moved away from the image of the President. The screen shifted to a brief shot of Representative John Lewis, the man there that morning who was most symbolic of the progress that separates our generation from the one just before it.

Instantaneously, I felt a vital part of this historic moment. When the man who had told me stories of being jailed, beaten, and harassed was pictured alongside our President at his inauguration, I finally understood how I was connected to these events. The Congressman's call to service that I had heard throughout my summer working in his office finally resonated within me, as I recognized the immense impact I could have on others. My experiences in DC had led me to young students struggling to survive in the juvenile justice system; to policymakers in the Congressional Black Caucus; to judges at the local landlord-tenant court. My diverse experiences and unique perspective could make me the compassionate, clear-minded leader that I felt called to be in those moments.

As we headed home that afternoon, this moment of inspiration settled deep into my thoughts as I began to reflect on my future. I knew I might never speak before millions on the Mall, nor would I likely ever face the kinds of brutality that the Congressman overcame. Like him, however, I do recognize the potential that lies in every person: the interwoven fabric of humanity that threads all of us together. In those moments and today, I feel a duty to strengthen this common identity, and I am ready to explore how I will best be able to do that.

WRITER'S WORDS OF WISDOM

Law school rankings are important, but you can also set yourself apart by doing well academically at law school. So even if you don't get into your dream school, you generally will still have great job opportunities if you study hard and excel in your classes.

CHAPTER
10

Georgetown University Law Center
Transfer Application

I always go beyond the "extra mile." As a marathon runner, when the task calls for determination and commitment, I go the full 26.2. Challenging myself and working hard for my goals takes me out of my comfort zone and into the greater world, and delving into the world around me ultimately led to my passion for women's empowerment work in developing countries. My experiences so far in law school reinforced my desire to work for women's rights, and I want to transfer to Georgetown University so I am best able to prepare myself to be part of the global effort for change.

As I considered international development work as a career, I wanted to better understand how progress in poorer countries worked, so I

CONVEYING LEADERSHIP

If you can think of a time when you saw a problem, figured out how to help address the situation, and gathered people behind you, this may be your ideal essay topic. The author chooses an excellent example for representing her leadership skills.

decided to experience it firsthand. I joined the Peace Corps, moved to the Kingdom of Tonga in the South Pacific, and began life in one of the more remote villages in the country. I knew that I would face more hardships living in a remote area, but I would get a better insight into the Tongan way of life than if I stayed in a bigger town.

While living on an island with 350 Tongans and no other foreigners, I became more than a bystander to life in a developing country; I became part of the community and culture. When I was not teaching at the local primary school, I was often with the women, helping them finish their tasks of cooking and cleaning, washing and weaving. From these daily interactions, I learned about the women's lives, and I heard their stories, both good and bad. Women told me of spousal abuse, teenage girls marrying for a financially secure future, and coerced marriages. I saw that, to improve these women's lives, they needed a voice in the community and for that they needed education and economic opportunities. Several of my projects worked to give women and girls the education and financial strength to be independent.

One of these projects was directing my island group's week-long girls' leadership camp. The national director of the camp asked me to organize the camp in my area, not just for my leadership and organizational skills, she said, but also because I knew how to work within the Tongan culture. As I began planning, I decided I did not want to simply repeat last year's camp. From my experiences in my village, I knew how important this camp was to giving girls their independence. This camp would be the first, and perhaps the only, opportunity many girls would have to discuss issues such as women's rights, domestic violence, alcoholism, and career opportunities. Because the camp could truly make an impact, camp planners and I decided to double the camp's size and create a framework to make the camp sustainable by making it entirely Tongan run.

In particular, working with community leaders, I formed a local planning team that would be involved in each step of the planning and implementation process and therefore would be prepared to lead the camp in the future. My team and I created a budget and led the necessary domestic and international fundraising efforts so girls could attend the camp regardless of their families' financial situations. People often did not understand the idea of a sleep-away camp, much less "girls' leadership," but we convinced parents to allow their daughters to attend by earning the support of influential community members.

The results of the camp proved the challenges worthwhile. At the closing ceremony, the girls performed plays that they wrote about what they had learned and eagerly talked of helping plan the next year's camp. High school principals started sexual health classes after seeing the importance of this information during the camp. One of our counselors even returned to high school to finish her degree. Our campers, almost half the 13- to 14-year-old girls on the islands in the area, are now better able to reach their goals and provide for themselves.

Choosing to push myself further and going beyond the "extra mile" got me involved in the Tongan culture, brought me to the women of Tonga, and led to our success at the girls' leadership camp. Although I had always supported women's rights, only through hands-on participation did I realize I want this to be the focus of my life's work. My experiences and dedication will take me further than the "extra mile" throughout my career, and Georgetown will take me further in my work for women's empowerment in developing countries.

I look forward to taking advantage of all Georgetown University offers to progress women's rights. Meaningful change comes from experience and knowledge. From working at the Women's Human Rights Clinic to learning from professors who are active in the work I intend to do, Georgetown will give me that experience and knowledge to truly make a difference. Success in women's empowerment requires dedication for the long run, and I am ready for that marathon.

CHAPTER

11

American University Washington College of Law

The first time I entered a library I was concurrently exhilarated by the immense vault of knowledge before me and overwhelmed by the realization that I could never consume it all. I wanted mastery over the stacks of books, but recognized that individually I was capable of only so much. I was and still am limited by my time and talents. Over the next decade, I found the solution to my predicament as I began to realize the power of the many over the individual. My greatest strength became my ability to enable others to reach their fullest potential and to organize a team toward a shared goal.

Two experiences brought me to these realizations. The first is the sport of rowing. At Georgetown, I have rowed on the varsity lightweight crew team for 4 years. The mechanics of rowing rely on a concert of competing forces. In our eight-man boat, the four port rowers pull from the left, creating a force that pushes against that of the four starboard rowers, pulling from the right. As the forces meet, they propel the boat forward toward the finish line. The second experience has been my work with Wikipedia. This platform engages in "crowdsourcing," the practice of outsourcing a project or problem to the crowds. It harnesses the power and wisdom of many contributors and focuses it toward the common, unified goal of creating an encyclopedic-type entry.

CRAFTING A MULTILAYERED FRAMEWORK

Focusing on one theme, the author manages to draw on multiple experiences that fit within the structure that he created. This is no easy task, but in this case, the author is able to pull it off as a result of his well-chosen theme of competing forces.

In a Wikipedia article, a number of collaborators with different perspectives and interpretations spar to create the most complete version of an entry. Both rowing and Wikipedia leverage the power of competing forces and derive their strength from the many. If only one rower were to pull hard, the boat would veer off course. If only one contributor were to write an article, the entry would lack completeness.

I believe that our judicial system is fueled by similar principles of competing forces and also derives its power from the contributions of many. The Constitution itself depends on the constant influx of great minds competing for successful interpretation and amendment. In the courtroom, adversarial competition works to bring justice to the surface. For my senior thesis in American Studies, I am proposing a theoretical enhancement to our current public defense system. Often, a public defense does not compete with the same force as a private defense. In an effort to resolve this discrepancy, I propose the option of having a defense "by the public." In a platform similar to Wikipedia, volunteers could brainstorm together, building the most concrete argument for the defense. Students, professors, and all interested parties could unite and through competition produce a powerful, balanced, and complete argument. The responsibility of the public defender would now be to mediate between the public and the courtroom, and to deliver the product that the crowds have produced. This process leverages competing forces and harnesses the power of the many toward a more complete justice. Most importantly, this enhancement would benefit the less fortunate by producing a more equitable system.

I hope to go to law school to acquire the skills I need to effect the positive societal changes I feel deeply responsible to produce. I fully grasp the power of the many over the individual and plan to apply this knowledge to my study and practice of the law. Ultimately, I aspire to become a force that competes with the great legal minds of past and present, and to interpret the law in a way that allows justice to prevail for all.

CHAPTER

12

Harvard Law School

While working as an intern at the World Service Authority this past year, I received a phone call that I will certainly never forget. In hesitating, heavily accented English, the man on the other end of the line said he urgently needed my help. Immediately setting to work to do just that, I spent the next few months striving to reach my goal of providing this individual with support.

In every aspect of my life, I firmly adhere to a belief in hard work. Though I may not always accomplish the exact result for which I am hoping, I have nonetheless found that my input is consistently proportional to the output I receive in the end. Last fall, I experienced the translation of this personal philosophy into tangible results through an internship that enabled me to observe the good I can achieve as a consequence of my own determination. Though I worked on behalf of an individual on whom I had never laid eyes, he, in turn, helped to confirm my desire to pursue a legal career directed toward social justice.

> **WRITER'S WORDS OF WISDOM**
>
> After reading your personal statement, the admissions officer should have a real sense of YOU.

As an intern with WSA, I had the unique opportunity to help craft legal strategies to advise our clients on reclaiming their human rights. While not an attorney dispensing advice or representing a client, I had the responsibility of developing creative solutions to difficult situations, and that man on the other end of the line presented me with one such dilemma.

After a half-hour phone call in which I heard the harrowing story of a young Iranian Christian forced to flee his birth country for the Netherlands, I set to work to do everything in my power to achieve justice for this desperate individual. Having been denied asylum in the Netherlands after exhausting his local legal remedies, he feared deportation to Iran. Simply put, my task was to determine a course of action to avert this.

Yet I quickly realized that there was much I did not know. I had a limited understanding of the European Council on Human Rights, I was unsure of the European Union's citizenship regulations, and I knew little about Dutch law. But rather than become disheartened by my lack of knowledge, I was inspired to learn. Although I have always loved learning for learning's sake, this case provided me with an opportunity to learn in order to make a difference in someone's life, and that fact made the challenge all the more stimulating. Despite the deficiencies in my knowledge, I was certain that I had the motivation to learn all I could in order to develop an effective strategy to prevent this man's deportation. With a refilled coffee mug and an endless supply of determination, I sat down to think, research, and think some more.

In the end, my hours of brainstorming, reading, and re-reading paid off, as my hard work uncovered the potential for this individual to apply for Dutch citizenship on the basis of family reunification. In our final phone call, my client, upon realizing he would likely be able to remain in the Netherlands, offered me the greatest reward I could have hoped for; he simply said "thank you." With those two words I was aware that the output of this experience had certainly matched my input to the case. Though there was no A+ or paycheck at the conclusion of this assignment, I received a far more valuable form of compensation, as I was instead rewarded with the confirmation that I had helped a man in need. While for me, understanding the causes of the French Revolution or the subplot of a Victorian novel are rewards in and of themselves, my internship with the World Service Authority provided the more tangible recompense of seeing the positive change my achieved knowledge had brought about. Accordingly, this experience has further reinforced my desire to pursue legal studies in order to gain the necessary tools to ultimately serve as a lawyer whose work contributes to the common good.

Regardless of the type of law I choose to practice, my actions will unavoidably affect human lives, and as someone who deeply cares about all that I do, I greatly look forward to that challenge. While I am not so naïve as to believe that things always turn out as I hope, I know I will consistently be able to rest with the knowledge that I have done my best in whatever it is I seek to achieve.

REVIEWING YOUR WORK

Proofread! Go beyond the basic spellcheck and ensure your essay is grammatically sound, as this author has done. Do you end any of your sentences with a preposition? Do you maintain subject verb agreement? Do you avoid passive voice? If you are applying to graduate school years after college, it will pay off to revisit these basic grammar rules not only for the sake of the personal statement but also for the writing tasks that await you in graduate school.

CHAPTER 13

Boston College Law School

My interest in law, particularly the international and immigration aspects of the legal system, began at an early age. The 5 years that I lived in Dublin, Ireland, made me acutely aware of the world beyond America's shores. I realized that a decision made in Washington could have a marked impact on another country. I visited Belfast and saw firsthand the deep segregation between Protestants and Catholics, and the effects of years of that violent struggle were startling. Yet these troubles have largely subsided, in part because of international influence and pressure.

My interest in international affairs, particularly the international legal system, was heightened during my junior year of college spent studying in London. I met students and professors who made me realize how English, Chinese, and American students are truly interconnected, and the importance of understanding each culture in order to have intelligent, enlightened debate and discussion. I studied international law and international organizations from an English perspective that served as a valuable contrast to what I had studied in the U.S. I have also taken courses focusing on the practice of diplomacy and the ethics of international relations. Entering into the legal profession seems like the next best step to turn this academic focus into a policy influencing reality.

My curiosity about the intricacies of both international and domestic law was also heightened in the past year because of two experiences with immigration in the U.S. My sister, a teacher in a New York City public high school, had an incredibly bright student who wanted to go to a top private university and was accepted. From my sister's stories and my encounters with him when I helped with Saturday tutoring my freshman year of college, I knew he would make a wonderful addition to any campus. He is not an American citizen, and therefore was not eligible for much financial aid. Unable to afford a private university on his own, he and his family spent months worrying about this predicament. Luckily he was able to work out an arrangement with a first-class university, and to the benefit of all the college students, he is on campus this year. I believe that it should not be this difficult for a hard working, intelligent student in America to get a first-rate education. Perhaps a couple of changed laws could fix this large problem.

COMBINING GLOBAL WITH LOCAL

The author describes large-scale international problems while also ensuring she brings attention to what this means to her on a personal level, while tying both into her ambitions of obtaining a law degree.

I was also struck by the injustices and intricacies of the immigration dilemma in the U.S. during my time as an employee at a food manufacturing company. This has been my summer job for the past four summers, and one of the most interesting aspects of the job is the people with whom I work. Although most of the people who work in the lab and the office are White Americans, the majority of workers in the plant doing the heavy lifting and making the product are Hispanic. The divisions that exist are not overt but still apparent. They are very hard working and without them the company would not function. Yet language barriers still exist, and it is difficult to become fully integrated into American society. The debate over immigration is often controversial, but it seems straightforward that everyone has certain rights that cannot be infringed upon regardless of their country of birth.

These experiences have greatly shaped my worldview and form the basis of why I want to go to law school. The world of the 21st century is so globalized and integrated that we cannot afford to be insular. My time spent abroad and my experiences here in the U.S. have given me a very international outlook. These unique experiences led me to pursue studies relating to international politics and to concentrate on international law. I believe that law school would complement and enhance this academic background and allow me to develop the skills to move from the academic realm to policy-making. Studying law in Boston, one of the oldest cities in the U.S. and home to a wide variety of different people and cultures, would be both challenging and rewarding.

WRITER'S WORDS OF WISDOM

Make sure that you are positive that you want to be a lawyer before going to law school.

BUSINESS

CHAPTER
14

Harvard Business School

How does pursuing an MBA support your choices above?

The time is now for me to pursue an MBA from HBS because the music industry urgently needs a change in its business model. I am seeking the fresh leadership perspectives and diverse management skills needed to provide creative and strategic direction to an industry that has relied upon gut instinct to sell music. By returning to a large record label and then perhaps starting my own, my goal is to use my leadership, artistic, and analytical abilities to improve the economics of the music business.

Tell us about something you did well.

When I first interned at Interscope Records, I quickly learned that its once foolproof methods of marketing music were no longer relevant in the rapidly digitizing landscape of music consumption. The company had access to exclusive and proprietary digital analytics such as Twitter mentions but it had no way of interpreting the data. Brooke Michael, Interscope's SVP, learned that I graduated as a math major and one day asked me to explore patterns in some of our data dashboards. I immediately realized that this was an opportunity to shake things up at the label by using the digitization of music to our advantage rather than to our detriment.

That month, I spent many late nights working to establish a system that would allow us to study music consumption patterns on the Internet in a more sophisticated way. Since we spent the most money on creating and marketing music videos, I decided to track how music video releases impacted 10 different metrics for a set of 80 artists. Organizing the data this way revealed many findings, such as that the rate at which fans search for a video on YouTube is directly correlated to the rate at which fans stream the song on Spotify. My analysis showed us that digital data had the potential to unlock crucial information about our artists' potential success rates in the market.

This exercise marked the first ever attempt to meaningfully navigate big data for the company. At the end of the summer, Brooke offered me a job to manage the data analysis process for product managers, brand partners, and even senior executives. The reporting system I created helped the Digital Department allocate a larger marketing budget to those artists whose videos were driving traffic to sales and also place a larger importance on Spotify since the data highlighted its value.

Over the past 2 years, I was promoted again to Senior Analyst and I now run the newly founded Analytics Group at the company. I have worked hard to train our team to use and expand upon the models I developed and as a result, we have been able to transform Interscope's marketing spend, moving the label from a push strategy to a fan-centric pull strategy. I am proud to have significantly advanced the company's efforts to sell music in a more relevant, effective, and cost-efficient way.

Tell us about something you wish you had done better.

In the spring of 2011, I created Washington, DC's first all-women's drumming festival called Rad Ladies That Drum. As a drummer, a gay woman, and a Women's and Gender Studies minor, the event marked a coming of age for me. For the first time, I was able to use my music as a social enterprise by providing 110 women ages 9 to 67 with an exhilarating space to demonstrate their knowledge in jazz, gospel, batá, go-go, rock, and djembe drumming. My goals for the festival were to inspire more women to play, to dispel stereotypes about women's drumming ability, and to empower women to seek out the toughest and most lucrative of gigs. Many people had tears in their eyes when we led the 600 audience members in a drum jam, concluding that soulful night in solidarity.

I originally thought that Rad Ladies That Drum would take place more regularly once I moved to LA. However, when attendees contacted me to ask if there were any future shows planned, I realized I had nowhere to point them. One of my deepest regrets is not giving direction to the momentum that had culminated with the festival. I was so passionate about the details of

WRITER'S WORDS OF WISDOM

The best two pieces of advice I could offer an applicant would first be to understand exactly what matters to them and second to sound warm and even informal in the essay. I had to take time to understand exactly what mattered to me before writing my essays so that my writing would be clear and honest. Then, I didn't have to fake some sort of wild story once it was clear what mattered to me (this could be anything!) because whatever I would write henceforth would be unique and a valid snapshot of my personality. When writing, I chose to be more warm and informal in my storytelling with the intention of offering up what was real. I chose not to be hyper sophisticated and formal, as taking that route risked the possibility of my essay sounding toneless and unmemorable.

planning and curating the festival that I did not lay the groundwork for future leadership.

I have thought deeply about how starting something powerful without ensuring its continuity can make a movement seem inconsequential and even hopeless. I loved that festival so much but realized that one person's vision alone is often not enough to sustain long-term change. Since my objective was to expand the presence of women in DC's music community, I should have engaged fellow drummers in planning the

festival with me so that Rad Ladies That Drum could continue to happen even in my absence. I realized that encouraging each individual to take a personal investment in the project would have allowed the complex planning process to belong to everyone and thus be more self-sustaining.

I am lucky to have learned this lesson so early in my career. As the first digital analyst hired at Interscope, I am working to build out an entire analytics department that will continue to advise digital strategy should I leave in the fall. Transitioning from an individual contributor to being an empowering teammate continues to be a cornerstone of my personal and professional endeavors today.

CHAPTER
15

University of California, Los Angeles
Anderson School of Management

What event or life experience has had the greatest influence in shaping your character and why?

Route 404 is a nondescript 75-mile expanse of rural highway from central Maryland, across the state of Delaware, stretching to the Atlantic shore. I first encountered Route 404 shortly after my 16th birthday. I accepted a dare from my older brother—"Can you bike to the beach?"— got on a rusty mountain bike, and started pedaling alongside him. The trek was 100 miles, but my journey was just beginning. The trek down Route 404, more than any other event in my life, has shaped my character.

The journey down Route 404 has given me the confidence and determination to take risks

> **WRITER'S WORDS OF WISDOM**
>
> If you are smart and hard working, your success in life won't be defined by which MBA program you went to. Don't get hung up on one school or another. You will end up where you need to be.

and face daunting challenges head-on. It has taught me the essence and value of teamwork. Most importantly, Route 404 has given me the perspective and purpose to recognize my own responsibility to society. The trek down Route 404 has shaped my life, and is embodied by my nonprofit, Bike to the Beach, Inc. (B2B): an organization that empowers and inspires others to dare greatly, to work as a team, and to change the world.

Challenges

That first year in 1999, fueled by adrenaline, I breezed through the first 25 miles. Then, as we rode onto Route 404, the ride shifted gears; the adrenaline wore off, the August heat beat down, and it seemed as if it was just me, my bike, and Route 404 stretching interminably eastward toward the glaring sunrise on the horizon. I have never endured more intense pain—physical or mental—than I did over those ensuing 8 hours. Determined to reach my goal, I exhausted every ounce of energy, willpower, and perseverance I could muster, and eventually, I arrived at the beach, delirious and beaten. I stumbled off the bike, collapsed into the salty ocean, and realized . . . I could not wait to do it again the next year!

On Route 404, at age 16, I learned that challenges allow us to tap into deep reservoirs of potential (physical, mental, and emotional) and attain lofty goals in the face of impossible odds. I learned that with initiative, vision, and resilience, I can overcome any challenge and find inspiration and true fulfillment in the process.

> **ESTABLISHING MOTIVATION**
>
> Providing insight into what motivates you allows readers to gain a strong understanding of your character. Here, the author succeeds at selecting an outstanding theme that represents his entrepreneurial nature, his ability to overcome challenges, and his commitment to his cause.

Teamwork

Each year since that first ride, my brother and I have invited friends, relatives, and strangers to join our annual "Bike to the Beach" challenge. Each summer, as riders face the challenge of Route 404, exhaustion sets in, and a genuine team is forged. Energetic riders sacrifice their personal goals, selflessly decelerate to allow struggling riders to draft behind them, shielded from the brutal headwind. The struggling riders are empowered, and the chain reaction extends from one rider to the next. This is no ordinary bike race; there is an undeniable team atmosphere. At the finish line, there is no personal glory; the struggle and the triumph are shared by the team as a whole.

On Route 404, I've witnessed genuine teamwork: miraculous moments, when individuals work selflessly, tirelessly, side-by-side, and the potential of the whole expands well beyond the sum of its parts.

Community

In 2006, while I was a senior at Georgetown University, my cousin was diagnosed with autism. Determined to join the fight against autism, I looked no further than Route 404. I transformed what had been an annual bike ride into a nonprofit organization, Bike to the Beach, Inc. (B2B), to raise awareness and money for autism. B2B's efforts culminate annually with the Bike to the Beach for autism century ride, and Route 404 is its centerpiece. For 4 years, I have built B2B into a thriving organization, as B2B has raised more than $750,000 for autism aware-

> **WRITER'S WORDS OF WISDOM**
>
> While in school, take every opportunity to get off campus and network with people in the industry you are interested in. Your ".edu" e-mail address will give you a free pass to almost anybody. Don't limit yourself to alums of your program, although they are a good place to start. Don't just think about what's-in-it-for-you when you meet with these people. Find out if you can help them. Prove to them you are a hardworking, reliable, proactive, positive, thoughtful person. Those relationships will be the most valuable things you graduate school with. Unless you are going to school for the love of books, you are getting your MBA to advance your career. Those relationships will help you in your career far more than any classes, extracurriculars, etc.

ness and research. More importantly, B2B has recruited and empowered more than 1,000 riders and volunteers to become involved in the fight against autism.

In life, everyone faces their own personal Route 404, whatever it may be. In moments of great struggle B2B riders find inspiration and empowerment both in each other and in the knowledge that they are supporting families around the country as those families face their own metaphoric Route 404: autism.

As an unpaid nonprofit entrepreneur, Route 404 has taught me the value of sacrifice to a cause and an organization. There have been moments of doubt, when I've considered that it wasn't worth the time and effort. In those moments, I remember my treks down Route 404, and I find strength, determination, inspiration, perspective, and purpose. Route 404 has deeply shaped my character, and in turn, I have characterized B2B as an organization that inspires and empowers others to dare greatly, to work as a team, and to change the world.

CHAPTER
16

University of Pennsylvania
The Wharton School

How will the Wharton MBA help you achieve your professional objectives?

There is a reason why President Obama's campaign for change in 2008 was a winning one. It struck a chord with Americans who were desperate after a decade of gridlock. The crushing realization followed that perhaps the promise of change was just "talk" and that things really cannot get done in Washington.

I was one of the Americans who had hoped for "change" and a new era of cooperation, but my hope slowly fizzled, and by the onset of the 2012 campaign, it had evaporated completely. The partisan finger-pointing and entrenchment stifled innovation and defeated ideas before they had a chance. All good policy starts with a visionary idea—like the New Deal and women's suffrage—but currently, what our country faces is not a lack of good ideas, it is an inability to implement them.

The skills missing from the equation are those that can take ideas and turn them into action, take strategy and transform it into reality, and I believe those are business skills. In 2 years at Google, I have seen firsthand how a successful business operates. Google values efficiency, productivity, and the promise of a new idea. I have learned that, to move anything forward, you have to do the legwork, get buy-in from stakeholders who often have competing interests, and above all else, execute well—and the same is true of policy making.

The Wharton MBA program will continue my education on what it takes to make an organization successful and how to be an effective leader. Wharton graduates can apply the skills acquired from the program to practical, real-life issues. Unlike many, I do not seek an MBA to work at a hedge fund or investment bank. I want to be a person who can take an idea and successfully turn it into something great. If admitted I would explore the Business and Public Policy major as a way to further understand their intersection.

> **ANTICIPATING THE QUESTION**
>
> Most graduate schools ask a more open-ended question; this specific essay prompt provides insight into what admissions officers are seeking. They want to see what else besides a commitment to academics prospective students would contribute to a given cohort. Admissions officers are looking to build a class; keep this in mind when writing an essay with any prompt.

At Wharton, the diversity and sheer number of classes, the emphasis on leadership, and the idea that the Wharton education does not end upon graduation are exciting and unique features of the MBA program. A Wharton education brings practical force to visionary ideals, and I plan to put my degree to good use. Our country needs policy leaders who can dream up the next big idea and execute it effectively—and I hope to be one of them.

Select a Wharton course, co-curricular opportunity or extra-curricular engagement that you are interested in. Tell us why you chose this activity and how it connects to your interests.

It would be an understatement to say that I was busy during my undergraduate years at Georgetown. I immersed myself in a variety of clubs and organizations that, while beautifully supplementing my academic life, certainly kept me active and mostly out of trouble. I managed a student-run snack shop (aptly called "Hoya Snaxa" in homage to our university), I was the Editor-in-Chief of a student newsmagazine, and I helped run new student orientation. Though I loved my classes and knew to prioritize my coursework, looking back I realize how academics formed only one part of my education. My extracurricular clubs and responsibilities, my friends and social life, together with my classes created a well-rounded, full education worthy of the financial investment.

When deciding whether to apply to Wharton's MBA program, I researched the classes I would be able to take, student testimonials about life at Wharton, and extracurricular opportunities, and tried to imagine what my life would be like on campus. I did so because I understand that, for me, education occurs in and out of the classroom. Along with taking core and elective classes, I want to feel engaged with the student body and feel like I am an important part of a community greater than myself. You've received my application because I am confident I would have that at Wharton.

From Women in Business to table tennis, Wharton offers an assortment of clubs and organizations all geared toward introducing students and enhancing campus life. The one club that excites me and that I will definitely join is the Politics and Public Policy club. Casual political conversation can be a dangerous minefield (my extended family is living proof of this). People become impassioned, stubborn, and unable to hear what others are saying. When the same debate is fostered within a willing, participatory group of people who simply want to share ideas and hear others, it can be an exhilarating experience. I am currently a member of a similar club in San Francisco and each month, I look forward to seeing the people who care enough about the issues that they not only encourage, but demand, respectful debate.

I have a lot to learn from Wharton. I know that I will be challenged by my classes, and I'm excited for that experience. The content of the classes will be completely new to me, and I'm eager to roll up my sleeves. However, I know from experience that there are more ways to be challenged and pleasantly uncomfortable while at a university. It's like jumping into the deep end, only half confident that you can swim. I am sure I will find common ground with fellow students in the Politics and Public Policy club, but I also know that I will test my personal limits and explore new interests while pursuing a Wharton MBA.

Imagine your work obligations for the afternoon were cancelled and you found yourself work free for three hours, what would you do?

COMMITTING TO SINCERITY

This statement speaks to the power of being completely genuine. The author could have suggested she would spend her time making investments or building up her business background; instead, the author gives an honest account of a leisurely afternoon exploring San Francisco, leaving readers with a strong impression of the candidate and an indication of the author's honest nature.

I live in a truly special part of San Francisco called Hayes Valley or, if you are a fan of the show *Full House*, right near the show's iconic pastel houses in Alamo Square. Rarely do I have the opportunity to enjoy my neighborhood in the calm of a workweek afternoon—when there are fewer tourists in Alamo Square, fewer runners in the Panhandle of Golden Gate Park, and fewer groups who love cheap weekend mimosas at my favorite cafe. I work an hour south of the city at Google's headquarters and, like many Bay Area commuters, dream of a free workday afternoon in the city. If given 3 afternoon hours off today, I would do the things I love most and recharge in my own pocket of San Francisco. First up—what will I cook for dinner?

My grocery list formulates as I walk up the stairs to my apartment. Down the hall and in my room, it solidifies. Brussels sprouts, my new favorite vegetable, make the cut. Chicken, maybe fish, because even with extra time, I am not terribly clever with a menu. And of course, a given for me, pasta in any form. I quickly change into my running clothes, slip my keys and a credit card into my pocket, and grab my old Winchester High School Tennis sweatshirt because, no matter the time of year, you need it in San Francisco. I rush out the door in hot pursuit of the last bit of sunlight on a sure-to-be foggy late afternoon. Some people fear running in San Francisco because of the many hills, but save one minimal hill, my chosen run through the Panhandle and into the park is purposefully flat. The route smells amazingly fresh due to countless eucalyptus trees and if I can make it all the way to the waterfall, past the de Young museum, I'll have experienced an unparalleled mental escape.

On the way home, I'll stop off at a market on Divisadero Street to collect my groceries and a few other things I won't have intended to buy but, of course, will. After a quick (read: very long) shower in my usually crowded apartment, I'll grab the new Erik Larsen book my Dad gave me that I haven't yet started and head to my favorite cafe for a few hours of peace and an out-of-this-world latte. By the time I return home to cook, my three roommates will be trickling in to share the remainder of my day.

It occurs to me that I ought to plan for rain, in which case, my backup to the run is to cross a movie off my growing list with a matinee or enjoy an episode or two of *The West Wing* from the couch. Everything else in my gifted afternoon remains the same — the cooking, the latte, and the untouched book. It won't be a crazy afternoon, but it will be perfectly and honestly me.

> **WRITER'S WORDS OF WISDOM**
>
> Reworking your essay too much or having too many reviewers can alter the tone and destroy what makes your essay yours.

Dartmouth College
Tuck School of Business

Why is an MBA a critical next step toward your short- and long-term career goals? Why is Tuck the best MBA program for you, and what will you uniquely contribute to the community?

What are the drivers of growth at a law firm? How do you model and capitalize on the relationship between service mix and profitability in a hospital system? How do you organize a global hospitality company for future growth?

These are only a few of the interesting challenges I have tackled as a consultant at a leading strategy consulting firm where, in few short years, I have learned more than I ever could have expected. The firm's apprenticeship-based approach to development has rapidly given me exposure to a wide range of industries and content areas. It has also enabled me to advance at my own pace. Last December, I was excited

WRITER'S WORDS OF WISDOM

It's helpful to create a matrix of characteristics the school values and the traits you want to communicate in your application. Then you can organize your content across essay questions and recommendations, checking off boxes as you go to ensure you don't leave any gaps.

to earn a promotion to Senior Consultant 6 months ahead of my peer group. Now, one month into my third year, I am approaching my first assignment in a manager role with enthusiasm and an open mind. I love my job, and I have no reason to believe that my trajectory will slow. That is why it is important to me at this point in my career to pause, reflect on my goals, and invest in an MBA to gain the leadership and general management skills that I need to achieve them.

After graduation, I plan to return to management consulting to solid-ify the skills I learn at Tuck before transitioning to an industry role as a cor-porate strategy executive. In order to be a successful leader of increasingly large, complex teams and, eventually, organizations, I need to develop positive leadership habits and establish a solid general management base. I am energized by Tuck's approach to leadership development, which bal-ances self-evaluation, classroom instruction, and coaching. Having time to reflect on my experiences and to receive guidance, both from faculty and from peers, will be invaluable to my development. Tuck's curriculum will allow me to build on the general management skills I was introduced to as an undergraduate and focus on the elective areas I value most: leadership, marketing, and strategy. In both leadership and general man-agement, I look forward to learning in 2 years at Tuck what would otherwise take a decade of trial-and-error to discover.

During my time in management con-sulting, I have been naturally drawn to Tuck alumni. They are, without fail, among the most thoughtful, capable, and fun individuals on any project team. I would be honored to be a part of that Tuck network, and in return I will dedicate my 2 years on Tuck's beautiful Upper Valley campus to creating innovative and lasting impact for future classes. At the firm, I changed the employee experience by founding the New York Training Initiative, a program designed

TAKING THE COMPATIBILITY TEST

The author brings up an excellent factor that played into her decision to apply to Tuck: the people. While many people take classes, professors, and career goals into consideration for their graduate school selections, the people with whom you will be going to school will inevitably play a big role in your experience, so it could be worth mentioning if that went into your decision making.

to expose employees to educational opportunities not addressed by the scope of their casework. At Georgetown's student-run credit union, I improved employee satisfaction by designing new standards and feedback systems. My involvement in and contributions to the Georgetown and my professional communities define who I am today, and I cannot wait to dive in at Tuck.

CHAPTER

18

Northwestern University

Kellogg School of Management and McCormick School of Engineering and Applied Science [Dual Degree]

Discuss moments or influences in your personal life that have defined who you are today.

A few days after graduation, I was sitting in Father Tom's office. Father Tom, a Jesuit professor whose course I took senior year, and I had formed a close relationship during our semester together. As a "thank you" for making such a positive impact on me, I came to his office that day to give him a present, a custom-made book of photos that I had taken around Georgetown's campus. As he finished paging through the book, he reached into his desk and pulled out a small card. It turns out

Father had a present for me as well, something that was much more meaningful than the book of photos, and something that would help me reach an important realization in my life. It was a business card that had my name on one line; on the second line, where a professional title would normally be positioned, it simply said "Human."

While we sometimes categorize ourselves as consultants and engineers, students and teachers, or husbands and wives, we all have the struggle of being human in common. This moment with Father helped me realize that my own human struggle—how I had worked to define myself—had been about finding an internally consistent picture of myself among the competing influences I had experienced up to that point.

I grew up in West Virginia as part of a large Italian family and attended Catholic school until eighth grade. I then received a full scholarship to a military academy in the Midwest, where I would spend my high school years. To say the least, my upbringing was spent in a conservative, often black and white world. I, in the meantime, was trying to make sense of the shades of gray I was personally experiencing. While living in the heart of the American Midwest, I was drawn to volunteering and studying in Bulgaria, China, and Russia. As I was struggling to understand my Catholicism and working my way through the institution's military leadership system, I was also working my way through accepting being gay. And, at Georgetown, I was struggling to align my academic focus on international politics with my desired pursuit of a career in business. Needless to say, these competing influences, environments, and identities did not sync up in any obvious way.

I have worked hard to be committed to recognizing what I'm good at (and what I'm not good at), adapting to changing worldviews, and engaging with others as genuinely as I know how. These commitments and convictions—formed in large part because of these competing influences—define the person I am today. Making

EXPRESSING A STRONG SENSE OF SELF

The author effectively weaves together a narrative that provides insight into a multifaceted individual; through the sincere writing style, the author is able to complete the difficult task of taking pride in his accomplishments while maintaining a humble demeanor.

sense of the various competing influences in my life was not always easy, but I am grateful for the experiences of each influence, because they have pushed me to gain strong self-awareness and inspired me to bring authenticity to all that I do.

I have learned that I must know and lead myself before I can successfully lead others. What excites me about the potential to be a part of the Kellogg and McCormick community is its same commitment to authenticity, as evidenced by the authenticity I see in every student or alumnus/a that I know. I believe that the MMM experience would push me to find new ways to act on my convictions, as I work to make an impact on the world around me.

WRITER'S WORDS OF WISDOM

Have multiple conversations with people who know you very well from different parts of your life. Your goal is to communicate what is uniquely interesting and valuable about you as a candidate. Figuring out how you are unique is not something you can do on your own, so ask others, and ask them explicitly.

19

London Business School

Essay 1: In what role or sector do you see yourself working immediately after graduation? Why? How will your past and present experiences help you achieve this? How will the London Business School MBA Programme contribute to this goal?

In the short-term, I plan to pursue a position in the field of corporate social responsibility with an international company. I am particularly interested in working with a food or beverage company to address agricultural sustainability, help improve environmental management, and promote social and economic development in local communities.

As Assistant Director of Buffalo ReformED, a Buffalo, NY-based education reform nonprofit, I researched and developed solutions to challenges in the local education system and worked with a diverse group of community members and business and political leaders to push for change within the system. This experience will prepare me to coordinate with individuals and agencies in both the public and private spheres and tackle the challenges involved with changing business practices to increase social impact.

I began working with Buffalo ReformED in its early stages. As the current Executive Director, I have had the opportunity to stabilize and improve the organization. I worked collaboratively with board leadership to establish a stable funding stream, a cohesive strategic plan, and a strong mission. This experience provided me with skills necessary to implement organizational change and enact innovative solutions that support both the business and the community it impacts.

While I have a strong background in the social sector, I believe an MBA at London Business School will provide me with the skills, tools, and international networks necessary to reach my goals and transition into the business world.

The core curriculum at LBS and flexibility offered through electives such as Social Entrepreneurship, Sustainability, World Problems, and Prospects will give me the diverse skill set necessary to work in a field that requires traditional business skills, entrepreneurship, and experience with public policy. The opportunity to specialize in a field such as change management would provide me with the skills necessary to shift a company's business practices in a way that enhances its social and economic impact.

A necessary skill in working in the field of corporate social responsibility is the ability to change attitudes and gain support for new ideas. London Business School's focus on building leadership and communication skills through

---

WRITER'S WORDS OF WISDOM

Graduate school is a major personal, financial, and professional investment. Before you embark on the application process, I would suggest some serious soul searching. I applied to graduate school for art history just after college; after spending time, energy, and money applying, I was accepted into a great program. At the same time, I had begun an exciting job with an education start-up and quickly realized that my career goals and aspirations had changed drastically. I decided not to pursue the MA in art history and instead focus on my new career. A few years later, I realized I wanted to hone my business acumen so that I could one day start my own entrepreneurial endeavor. This led me to apply to business school. Half a year into my MBA

continues on page 81

the Leadership Launch and Global Leadership Assessment for Managers will prepare me to take a leadership position in an international setting, communicate ideas effectively, and influence others.

An MBA from the London Business School will help me reach my goal of working with an international company by providing unique opportunities to connect with a diverse and international student body and extensive alumni network and gain hands-on experience through a study abroad program or Global Business Experience.

As an American student with an international background, I am seeking an MBA experience in London because I believe it will be the best platform from which to pursue my goal of increasing social impact in the business world. The LBS MBA will provide me with the right skills, the most diverse network and the most challenging environment in which to develop; in return, I will be a valuable resource and active addition to its community.

continued from page 80

program, I'm sure I've made the right choice to pursue this path, although it was a windy road getting here! The decision to apply to grad school should be well thought out and planned in advance. Give yourself time to talk to current students, and research potential career paths. Don't just apply because you think you should or because you're struggling in the job market.

Essay 2: Where do you see your career progressing five years after graduation and what is your longer term career vision?

After working in the corporate responsibility branch of an international company for 5 years, I aim to have completed projects that build socially responsible practices within areas such as environmental sustainability or agricultural development.

Through these experiences, I will build the skills necessary to launch my own social venture—a recycling company that aims to promote recycling and decrease pollution in Cairo, Egypt. During my travels to Egypt, I noted that waste disposal practices are primitive, and recycling of plas-

KNOWING YOUR AUDIENCE

The author realizes the program's emphasis on leadership development and addresses this by providing examples of her professional leadership and communicating her desire to further enhance her skills.

tics and other reusable materials is very limited. I plan to launch a company that gives incentive to individuals to recycle by offering them monetary rewards, while providing cheaper recycled materials to local manufacturers. If successful, this model would create economic benefit for urban individuals, while changing attitudes toward environmental sustainability. I plan to incorporate a strong community education component in order to enhance the company's impact and empower local citizens to engage in efforts to improve their environment and quality of life.

Business models that integrate social and commercial value are a relatively new frontier, especially in nations like Egypt. I aim to be a leader in this field, supporting creative and sustainable solutions to social and environmental problems.

Essay 3: Give a specific example of when you have had to test your leadership and/or team working skills either professionally, or outside of work. What role will you play in your first year study group?

In December 2010, I was appointed to the advisory board of the New York Campaign for Achievement Now, an education reform organization dedicated to improving New York State's public education system. The advisory board consists of educators and leaders who hold different ideas on public education reform.

My first task was helping to decide the policy goals for 2011. The challenge of balancing diverse opinions proved difficult; rather than collaborate productively, each board member used the opportunity to advance his own cause. We needed to work together in a way that focused on the organization's mission as a whole. Instead of allowing the members to lobby for individual goals, I asked each one to provide a single legislative item that would be most impactful for the organization. When we listed the priorities, the group was surprised to see that there was considerable overlap. With that in mind, it was much easier for us to reach consensus. I created a ranking rubric that optimized impact and feasibility, and eventually the group agreed on three top priorities.

This experience taught me a valuable lesson about group work. If an assignment arises in which there is conflict over how to reach a solution, I will be able to balance differing opinions and find common ground. I am unafraid to take a leadership position and have strong organizational and time management skills. At the same time, I recognize that being a part of a successful team requires encouraging others to take ownership and initiative.

PAYING ATTENTION TO DETAIL

The author succeeds in identifying an experience that addresses the prompt and provides ample details in terms of how she was able to demonstrate leadership.

I have learned that the LBS study group is more than an academic group; it becomes a family and support network. As a socially adept and outgoing person who thrives in new environments, I will be able to facilitate relationship building and an effective working environment within my group.

Essay 4: Student involvement is an extremely important part of the London MBA experience and this is reflected in the character of students on campus. What type of student club or campus community events will you be involved with and why? How will you contribute?

Throughout my life I have always sought to be an active and giving member of the communities to which I belong.

I have volunteered with mentoring and tutoring programs for over 5 years. I hope to continue this work at LBS by participating in tutoring programs in Westminster. I currently volunteer with the Georgetown University Alumni Admissions Program and can apply this experience to help support CV writing sessions or interview practice for youth in the community.

I have played football for most of my life, though I've always called it soccer, and would be eager to join the Women's Football team, bringing athletic and team leadership skills with me. As an undergraduate I founded an art appreciation club at my university. We organized events and trips to nearby museums. I hope to contribute to the Art Appreciation club at LBS by utilizing these skills to help organize events and increase student participation. I am an avid drum player and would be interested in connecting with other musicians through Music Club. I am passionate about cooking; I would like to find or found a club that celebrates the student body's diversity through international cuisine.

I am interested in exploring my professional interests and networking with peers through the Responsible Business Club. As the Executive Director of a nonprofit organization, I believe I can offer a unique perspective on the social sector. I would seek new challenges through participation in the Global Social Venture Fund competition.

I hope to be an active member of the student community through participation in clubs and social events such as Tattoo, or the annual Snow Club ski trip. I am eager to interact with my peers, learn from their diverse experiences, and use my previous experiences and leadership skills to strengthen the LBS community.

Essay 5: London Business School offers a truly global and diverse experience. Describe any significant experiences outside of your home country or culture. What did you gain and how will your experience contribute to the School?

In 2008, I participated in a 6-month study abroad program in Seville, Spain. I lived with a Spanish family and took courses taught fully in Spanish at the Universidad de Sevilla, alongside students from Spain and other parts of Europe. The full immersion approach pushed me to adapt to a different culture and academic style. Beyond Spanish language skills, studying abroad gave me an opportunity to experience a new culture and evaluate myself and my role in a globalized world. As an American student in Spain, I pushed my own boundaries in order to integrate and communicate with my peers. As an international student with a nontraditional work background, I may face a similar experience at LBS. I will be able to capitalize on the differences in culture and experience that will surely exist between my classmates and me, enhance their network, and provide a unique perspective in the classroom.

Essay 6: Give an example of a person who, in your opinion, has made a profound impact on the way the world does business. How will this person influence your contribution to your MBA Programme at London Business School?

By bridging the gap between traditional banking and social good, economist and banker Professor Muhammad Yunus has profoundly impacted the way the world does business. In the mid 1970s, while visiting some of the poorest households in Jobra, Bangladesh, he discovered that small loans to village women could help them to overcome poverty. His personal loan to rural basket weavers in Jobra grew into Grameen Bank—a formal bank that continues to make momentous advances toward eradicating poverty through the concept of microlending.

Professor Yunus's impact on the business world has inspired my professional goals and will help shape my contribution to the MBA program at London Business School. Muhammad Yunus was one of the original social entrepreneurs; he challenged the idea that social good and economic benefit must exist in isolation. This type of thinking across sectors will drive my approach to the MBA experience. Finding solutions to complex issues, whether in the social or business realm, requires a combination of strategies and use of best practices from multiple sources. I will apply my professional experiences in the nonprofit world to the MBA curriculum in order to find unique solutions to academic questions and real world issues. I will be open to the ideas and perspectives of others.

Muhammad Yunus challenged the status quo in Bangladesh. He overcame political and social backlash to serve more than 7.5 million borrowers living in poverty. Despite Grameen Bank's nontraditional approach to lending, its business model has proven to be exceptionally successful, even by traditional metrics. Throughout my 2 years at LBS, I will challenge the status quo, ask questions, and take risks. I will take advantage of the diverse academic and extracurricular opportunities available to me in order to gain the skills necessary to make an impact in the business and social sectors.

CHAPTER

20

Northwestern University
Kellogg School of Management

Assume you are evaluating your application from the perspective of a student member of the Kellogg Admissions Committee. Why would you and your peers select you for admission, and what impact would you make as a member of the Kellogg community?

The students of the Kellogg Admissions Committee have accepted Jane into Kellogg's class of 2014.

We've selected her primarily because her energy and passion mirror our own. While all Kellogg applicants have proven records of intelligence, Jane merges intellect with authentic energy. She has an entrepreneurial spirit that breeds contagious excitement and drive for change. As evidenced by her team-based consulting work, she is collaborative and converts her ideas into building blocks for end solutions. Jane's pas-

DOING YOUR HOMEWORK

The author demonstrates that not only has she done significant research on her chosen program, but she also goes a step beyond to explain what she envisions herself doing upon arriving on campus and why she would be a strong fit.

sion for women's leadership is clear from both her ongoing work with Georgetown's Women in Business group and also in her desire to build a business that supports women's leadership across the world. The Kellogg culture is rooted in people with such deep passion; the vibrancy of our community comes from the diversity of focus, yet commonality of intensity in the passions of our students. Jane's energy makes her a natural fit into the Kellogg culture.

Additionally, we've selected Jane because we believe she will contribute meaningfully to Kellogg. It is clear that Jane understands the importance of both taking from and giving back to her school. That is, Jane will grab hold of all of the opportunities provided to people in purple. She will attend the Kellogg Super Bowl Ad Review, join the Kellogg Operations Seminar Series, and adventure across the world on a GIM trip. We also picture Jane giving back to Kellogg. Jane will lead a Neighborhood Business Initiative project, organize the Special K show, serve as a voice on the KSA, and run a KWEST trip. We can tell that Jane is like us; she pre-fers to be overcommitted and on the go. While at Georgetown, Jane threw herself into lead-ing groups and activities. She did the same at her consulting firm, chairing committees and leading the office in well being initiatives. We believe Jane will also do this at Kellogg by lever-aging her natural talent to build networks and to connect people. Not only do we view this talent as a powerful tool in business, but we also see this as a key to weaving the Kellogg community together to make us even stronger.

We also want to sit and have a beer with Jane. Business school is just as much about being tempered by peers in the day-to-day as it

WRITER'S WORDS OF WISDOM

Don't get too married to a paragraph or a sentence no matter how hard you've worked on it or how poetic it sounds. If people you respect read through your essays and don't understand what you're saying, don't try to convince them otherwise (you won't have this chance with an admission officer!). Just rewrite it to make sense and move on.

is learning from professors in classrooms. Jane has stories ranging from sleeping in chicken huts in rural Fiji to discussing diabetes prevention with health officials of the Middle East. She has stories about the broken health care industry and profit margins shrinking, executives coming under new microscopes and budget cuts quickly eradicating mission. She can share about her interests ranging from running half-marathons and powder skiing to collecting Absolut Vodka ads and the dramatic arts. We want to sit with her at a TG to laugh, brainstorm, and exchange our experiences and thereby enrich all of our perspectives.

Lastly, we've selected Jane because we know she will do great things with her life. We believe that after Kellogg Jane will launch into a lifetime of adventures and achievements. Jane has the unique gift to imagine avenues to create shared value and to weave together depth and conscience with profit and market share. Between her creativity and drive, she will build the business she has dreamed of and be a part of many more successful endeavors. Jane will be an alumna that is deeply proud of her Kellogg connection, and, in turn, we know Kellogg will be deeply proud of her.

WRITER'S WORDS OF WISDOM

Allow the essays to be a struggle. Going to grad school is a HUGE investment of resources and load of personal strain. The essays are meant to help you wrestle through your real "whys" for grad school. Going through the struggle, cliché as it sounds, will make you stronger and able to extract the most from school once you're there.

CHAPTER
21

University of California, Berkeley
Haas School of Business

1. If you could choose one song that expresses who you are, what is it and why?

In *Willy Wonka and the Chocolate Factory*, Wonka sings "Pure Imagination": "If you want to view paradise/Simply look around and view it." Although, unfortunately, our world is not comprised of chocolate rivers and schnozberries, it is, like Wonka's factory, an astounding place that excites my inner dreamer and explorer. What began as a teenager obsessed with rock climbing in the Northeast expanded to a global fascination with pushing my limits and exploring some of the most remote parts of the world. This year, I have SCUBA dived in Iceland, mountain biked in the Moab desert, and backpacked Alaska. However, simply exploring is not enough. Wonka expresses the importance of sharing these experiences: "Come with me/And you'll be/In a world of/Pure imagination." I push my friends and family to join me on these excursions and, in doing so, have grown closer in my existing relationships as well as have made many new ones. The global opportunities at Haas are one of the main reasons I am so excited about the program.

My passion for innovation and belief in creating my own destiny is also asserted in the lines "Anything you want to/Do it/Wanta change the world?/There's nothing/To it." Working hard to go from a walk-on on Georgetown's varsity baseball team to a 3-year starter while still being a cum-laude student and active Baker Scholar exemplifies my drive. This focus has now shifted toward pursuing an MBA at Berkeley where I will concentrate on global entrepreneurship with a goal to one day "change the world."

2. *What is your most significant accomplishment?*

This year my line manager acknowledged my productivity and growth and gave me my own account list ahead of schedule. What makes this my most significant accomplishment, besides the sped up timeline, is that I have also considerably increased revenues with these accounts in my first year and have already surpassed the productivity of many of my peers. For example, one of my derivatives account's volumes are up over 500% annualized in 2012 and Barclays has jumped to become their top-rated dealer. Now, the account does not even put us in competition with other dealers, which is a rarity in our business and a testament to the relationships that I have built with their traders. I have also received some challenging accounts; ones that were frustrated with Barclays in the past and had generally stopped trading with us. One index manager in Minnesota fit this description; however, within the first month of covering him, we printed a $20,000,000 trade, which was the largest trade any of my managers had seen from the account. He has remarked that his relationship with Barclays has been much better since we started working together. The successes that I have had so far with my account base have been very gratifying and the results have been my greatest accomplishment to date.

However, more important than my personal accomplishments has been the success of our Chicago rates team. The three of us in Chicago work seamlessly together and are currently way ahead of our 2012 revenue target, which is impressive given the current economic landscape.

3. Describe a time when you questioned an established practice or thought within an organization. How did your actions create a positive change?

Shortly after my move to Chicago with Barclays, the debt crises in Europe reemerged and created an unpredictable macroeconomic landscape that was susceptible to large swings from "headline risks." Due to the uncertainty, our traditional Chicago institutional clients moved their money out of the market and trading volumes fell. As a result, our Chicago team experienced declining activity and revenues.

Fortunately, my background was perfect for the changed environment. Hedge funds, which were my specialty in New York, thrive in times of uncertainty and market dislocation. I quickly proposed that we should react by diversifying our client base to include more hedge funds and proprietary trading shops. I had already developed a strong relationship with a proprietary trader in Chicago, and my age, experience in New York, and personality aligned perfectly with these accounts, so I was confident that our group could build more "fast-money" relationships.

My managers trusted me and either sent me by myself or took me with them to prospect new clients, an invaluable learning experience since it was something that no one my age was doing. We established relationships with many new accounts, immediately increasing our fast-money coverage more than 10 times in the first 6 months. As the European crisis hit its pinnacle through late 2011 and into 2012, trading volumes from our traditional Midwest clients dried up and our new clients were the drivers of our revenue. In fact, despite the volatile market we are still running at 130% of budget.

4. Describe a time when you were a study of your own failure. What specific insight from this experience has shaped your development?

The sole propeller in our Cessna-172 windmilled lifelessly in the wind as I ran through my emergency procedures. "Mayday, mayday," Matt, the pilot in the seat next to me, blurted over our radio.

A few hours earlier, I had been on the ground inspecting the plane to make sure it was safe for us to conduct our flight. The one red flag that I noted was that the fuel tanks were only half-filled. Doing some quick math, I calculated that the flight was doable, but without much room for error. When I pointed out our fuel situation to the pilot-in-command, he declared that there should be enough fuel for our flight, and we fired up the engine.

A few hours later we were forced to emergency land in a snowy backyard. Looking back on the situation, I had ignored my instincts and blindly accepted the pilot-in-command's analysis of our fuel situation based on his seniority and flight experience.

Since the crash, I have encountered many similar situations. At Barclays, I will routinely price trades and come up with a different result than a senior trader. The plane crash taught me to be confident about my judgment and not be afraid to push back on a superior in the proper situation; one memorable incident saved our company $50,000 on the pricing of an amortizing swaption. The crash also reinforced the importance of perseverance. Two weeks later I was back up in the sky, making that same flight, and I have since continued to achieve more advanced ratings and licenses.

5. a. What are your post-MBA short-term and long-term career goals? How have your professional experiences prepared you to achieve these goals? b. How will an MBA from Haas help you achieve these goals?

Ever since my early days of dissecting old computers with my dad, technology has fascinated me. Later, this hobby inspired a degree in computer science at Georgetown, the foundation of my website development company, and the start of the website I created. The time I spent brainstorming ideas for the website, watching it organically grow, and seeing it receive the second most hits on ABCNews.com, were some of my most fun and rewarding times. I am currently in the planning and development stages of a new website idea, which provides entrepreneurs with a "start-up lab" and a social matching service to investors, engineers, lawyers, and more. I plan to concentrate my studies at Haas in entrepreneurship with the goal to join an early stage technology start-up and eventually found my own.

Although my goal is to switch industries, my time at Barclays has provided me with essential skills that will aid this transition. I have found many parallels between growing my client portfolio at Barclays and the experience that I had starting my website design company. To increase market share, I have needed to be knowledgeable about my customer base, deliver thorough work in a timely manner, and work well with my teammates. My role at Barclays is also very client facing, and I have built the confidence to provide my market opinion and trade suggestions to some of the most important money managers in the Midwest. This has been effective training for when I will need to pitch to investors or eventually try to hire someone away from a competitor.

Barclays has also forced me to mature as a businessman in an extremely demanding environment. The head of my division was sure

TAKING ADVANTAGE OF ALL ASPECTS OF THE APPLICATION

The author later utilizes an optional essay form within the application's supplemental section in order to further describe the website he created so he is able to use his site to explain his point without having to go into too much detail here, as he thoroughly describes it elsewhere.

to remind me of this my first day, warning me that "there are no safety nets in trading" and that "every day could be your last." The work ethic and thick skin that I developed through decades of serious athletics has allowed me to succeed at Barclays. I know that if I can thrive in the fierce financial industry then I can work anywhere, so I am prepared to tackle any coming career challenges.

After Barclays, Haas will be a perfect progression for me both educationally and for my career. I elected to get a liberal arts degree at Georgetown because I knew I would later pursue an MBA. I have always had a very curious mind (my friends made fun of me for claiming that class selection time was one of the best times of the year), so the educational freedom at Georgetown College instantly appealed to me. The 12 core classes at Haas, such as financial accounting and strategic leadership, will allow me catch up on subjects that I forwent at Georgetown and that are essential for someone running his own business to take, while Haas' 60% elective curriculum will satiate my intellectual curiosity.

Furthermore, Haas' commitment to entrepreneurial studies, through classes such as the "Entrepreneurship Workshop for Start-ups," will provide the educational foundation to help jumpstart a technology start-up. In addition to all the noteworthy classes, the numerous extracurricular activities and support systems that Haas offers will help cultivate my entrepreneurial spirit. Contests like The Intel Global Challenge would evoke my competitiveness and the Lester Center and its offerings, such as Skydeck, the speaker panels, and the opportunity to work with Jeff Burton, are all invaluable experiences for budding entrepreneurs. Whether inside or outside the classroom, I am genuinely excited about the opportunity to study in the epicenter of innovation and learn from Haas' unparalleled faculty and staff.

Lastly, with the world becoming increasingly interconnected, it is clear that any future company will need to compete on a global scale. For instance, the new austerity measures in Europe should leave a lot of European entrepreneurs starved for a cheaper home to start and grow their business. Understanding foreign business practices will be crucial in effectively partnering with this market. I love that Haas encourages its students to learn abroad and am particularly excited about the IBD program, which would allow me to hone my innovative leadership skills on a global platform. I was unable to study abroad at Georgetown due to the yearlong commitment of a Division I sport, so I look forward to the international opportunities at Haas. Haas' complete curriculum will help me further develop the business skills that I learned at Barclays, fill in my education gaps from Georgetown, and provide a springboard for a career in technological entrepreneurship.

PRESENTING A WELL-ROUNDED APPLICANT

The author excels at choosing topics that reveal a dynamic individual and that achieve the goal of leaving the readers wanting more (in the best possible way).

CHAPTER 22

Duke University
Fuqua School of Business

When asked by your family, friends, and colleagues why you want to go to Duke, what do you tell them? Share the reasons that are most meaningful to you.

Three years ago, when I left a for-profit company to work for a non-profit organization, I heard many of the reactions that I now know are commonplace for those working in the social sector. I had friends declare, "Good for you!" as if I was pursuing some higher moral ground by taking a job with Teach For America. When I would catch up with former colleagues, the questions they would ask about my new job were more about how I liked the reduced hours than about the work I was doing. Overall, it seemed as if others perceived my career change as a personally beneficial decision, rather than a professionally driven one. To them, I looked like someone who couldn't necessarily hack the 80-hour work week and who wanted to save the world rather than be successful.

Though frustrating, this experience ultimately cemented my commitment to working in the social sector, rather than discourage it. In the eyes of my former colleagues, many among them future business leaders,

I saw a lack of respect for the work of solving social problems. The decision to make this work the focus of my career in spite of these challenges is not one I've taken lightly, nor is the decision to apply to Duke. I want to go to Duke because I believe that its faculty, students, and alumni think the same way I do about the social sector: that it needs and warrants the same level of talent as for-profit sectors in order for our global economy and society to thrive.

I first learned of Fuqua from a former manager at the consulting firm where I worked, who had collaborated with researchers at the Center for the Advancement of Social Entrepreneurship (CASE) for her recent book on high-performing nonprofits. At this point in my career I had just begun to discover my passion for helping nonprofit leaders make their organizations more effective, and when my manager mentioned the work of CASE, I realized that there were institutions out there dedicated to applying the same rigorous research and business methods to social issues as there were for consumer products or financial investments. As I explored Fuqua further, I saw that its students seemed particularly invested in integrating the work of social organizations and for-profit enterprises, judging by the fact that the MBA Net Impact Club is among the most popular on campus. Fuqua also seems deeply committed to developing socially conscious business leaders through its curriculum focus on ethical leadership and cross-cultural awareness. Finally, Fuqua's dedication to reducing financial barriers for students pursuing nonprofit careers is unparalleled and sends a clear message that channeling business acumen to the social sector is a major priority for Duke.

WRITER'S WORDS OF WISDOM

Ask anyone and everyone to read your personal statements and give you feedback. Writing about yourself in an honest, candid way can be really challenging, so making sure you are getting your point across to the reader is critical.

I have learned through my experience working in and consulting for nonprofit organizations that an integrated approach to solving social problems is best accomplished through adapting rigorous business practices with knowledge of the social context. At Teach For America, our relentless focus on measurement and data is adopted from the data-driven processes of many successful companies. We consistently measure nearly everything, from the achievement of students in our corps members' classrooms to donor satisfaction with our fundraising communications. However, I've seen that proposing a corporate top-down approach to implementing new initiatives does not sit well in our context, particularly because those who might technically be "low on the totem pole," our corps members, are the ones making the actual impact in classrooms. For this reason, I know that I need to pursue my MBA at an institution that understands the complexity of adapting business practices in the nonprofit setting so that these practices contribute to, rather than hinder, social change.

WORKING WITH WORD LIMITS

The essay's limitation in length leaves little room for providing all the details you might want the admissions officers to know about you. Note how in 818 words, the author succinctly and persuasively delivers insight into her career experiences, her goals, and her interest in attending business school.

I know that attending Duke and taking advantage of the many opportunities Fuqua offers would allow me to become the well-rounded social sector leader I need to be in order to really make an impact. Nonprofit success is undoubtedly tied to relationships with for-profit funders, government agencies, politicians, and high net worth individuals around the globe. Duke's global reach and focus would allow me to learn as much as I can from my diverse classmates and to benefit from their experiences across industries. Given that my short-term goal is to better understand the perspectives of high net worth donors, I feel that my work with this audience could only be enhanced by better understanding the business language they speak and applying this lens to nonprofit work. I would relish the opportunity to add my own perspective and experience to Duke's values-driven community, and in particular feel I would thrive in making connections with my classmates and Fuqua alumni that could prove beneficial to the organizations and social causes that I hope to eventually serve.

CHAPTER
23

University of Virginia
Darden School of Business

Share your perspective on leadership in the workplace and describe how it has been shaped by the increasing influence of globalization.

The best leaders for a globalized era develop their employees' creativity and facilitate a team atmosphere. I have seen such leadership in action at the Federal Reserve, where I have worked under leaders focused on developing an organization ready to create new solutions to unforeseen problems. I believe that developing a flexible organization, with employees who can work together to apply their skills to new challenges, is more critical now than ever.

Today's leaders must foster creativity both within themselves and their teams. One of the predominant trends of globalization has been the quickening of information diffusion, which has accelerated the speed at which organizations need to adjust to change. In a globalized

OFFERING EXAMPLES

The author successfully draws on personal work experience to support the claims made within the essay, which bolsters the argument and offers insight into the applicant.

environment, leaders cannot develop stationary organizations centered around their own decision making, but must encourage their employees to acquire analytical skills while retaining a flexible mindset to apply those skills to new areas. I have seen the benefits of such an approach at the Federal Reserve, since many of the ideas about what actions to take during the financial crisis were created not by working off of old ideas, but rather by defining goals and then considering what strategies, tested and untested, were most likely to reach those goals. Facilitating creativity is challenging, but leaders in a globalized environment must encourage their employees to consider problems from a variety of perspectives and question current modes of operation.

To succeed in a globalized era, leaders must also create a collaborative atmosphere. Having employees work together lets them learn from each other's skills, while also promoting productivity through specialization. Enabling employees to gain expertise and responsibility in a certain area lets them take advantage of their creativity to develop new perspectives and deeper knowledge of that sector. At the same time, a team atmosphere should encourage people to contribute in areas outside their expertise. By combining these two benefits of teamwork—using it to acquire new perspectives and skills, and then applying these to new areas—leaders can prepare businesses to compete in a global market.

I have seen leadership with these foci in practice: I believe that a large part of what makes my organization successful is that its leaders encourage people to work with others with different academic backgrounds, so that everyone is exposed to new ways of thinking about their work. Teamwork has always been important, but the best leaders in a global environment will develop employees with varied perspectives, specialized skills, and the ability to apply them to diffuse sectors of the business and broader econ-

WRITER'S WORDS OF WISDOM

The culture of the school is really important. Although it might be hard to find out what a school's culture is like before you enroll, it is worth spending some time to try. Culture will have more of an impact on your experience than any other factor. Darden's culture turned out to be great for me, but I should have given it more thought before going.

omy. In this way, leaders can prepare their firms for the novel challenges globalization will bring.

Leadership has always been critical to business success, but globalization has created new demands for managers in today's workplace. Today's leaders must focus not only on today's challenges, but also on developing creative, team-oriented organizations to face unpredictable obstacles. By doing so, they will position themselves to have long-term success in a globalized market.

CHAPTER
24

Harvard Business School

Answer a question you wished we asked.

Why am I a vegetarian?

I still crave bacon. A lot. Being a vegetarian for the past 7 years, however, has not only tested my principles daily but has also taught me the joy of being disciplined and true to my values.

I was always disturbed about animals kept in confined dirty spaces and subsequently killed. Nonetheless, I never let go of my Churrasco. A theology class discussion at Georgetown challenged my quickness to embrace instantaneous gratification and inspired me to act on my belief that imposing suffering on any living being is utterly unethical.

The temptations are many! Not long ago, I was at Casa, my favorite Brazilian restaurant in NYC, thinking how great the shrimp stew probably tasted. The waiter came back to the table twice before I could make a decision. Ultimately, I ordered the only vegetarian option, and it felt great. Nothing except my own conscience was stopping me from eating shrimp, and I was happy I had the discipline to stick to what I believe in. I wasn't going to compromise my values for a fleeting sensation.

All this said, I am not a proselytizing vegetarian! I won't send friends shocking videos of cows being slaughtered. I won't shove my values down others' throats. Instead, I influence people subtly, such as by cooking a delicious vegetarian meal for my friends and highlighting its health advantages.

To keep my belief in animal rights alive, I am the team leader for Added Value Farms, a sustainable urban farm located in Redhook, Brooklyn, an impoverished neighborhood that has no grocery stores and no place where the community can buy fresh vegetables. Every other Saturday, I lead 20 volunteers to complete tasks as varied as building planting beds, turning compost, and harvesting.

Through my work at the farm, I contribute to producing fresh vegetables for the Redhook community and spread the message about vegetarianism and the benefits of substituting meat consumption with cheaper, healthier, and sustainable options.

BEING TRUE TO YOURSELF

At first glance, one might ask what being a vegetarian has to do with being a strong candidate for business school. However, within this chosen focus, the author is able to present herself as someone who does not back down from her beliefs and who puts her thoughts into actions, which are attractive qualities in someone pursuing a career in business.

I shared this story because it represents one of the most challenging yet rewarding aspects of how I like to live my life. It's easy to ascribe to oneself values that haven't been tested; doing what one believes to be morally right is often extremely difficult. Yet, the choice to live up to one's values is one that we all have. I'm proud of myself because for the past 7 years, I have lived up to my belief that no living being ought to suffer. In different aspects of my life, personal and professional, I aspire to always be true to my values.

CHAPTER
25

Stanford Graduate School of Business

What do you want to do—REALLY—and why Stanford?

I have been very lucky to learn a tremendous amount and develop a strong set of skills while working within investment banking and investing roles over the past few years. However, the experience that I have gained has lacked one significant component: doing work that has a positive impact on people outside of my organization. I do not mean to imply that I feel like the career path I pursued negatively impacts society or that the investment bank and private equity firm I worked for do not do good things for their communities—I have been lucky to be part of several community service initiatives at both firms that have been extraordinarily successful.

Rather, I mean that the day-to-day work I am doing only has a tangential impact on a broader scale. The limited partners that have selected my fund as steward for their capital

> **KEEPING AN OPEN MIND**
>
> The author is candid about his ambitions and rather than expressing a desire for a particular career path, he reveals his intention to find fulfillment above all else. Embrace uncertainty.

110

love l

to

WRITER'S WORDS OF WISDOM

I think a lot of people write essays that are along the lines of "I want to do good in the world"... naturally, I would also like to achieve that goal. But I wanted to make sure that my essay wasn't focused on charitable work for the sake of impressing the reader—I wanted it to be an honest and a real representation of what I wanted. If that happens to be something philanthropic, great, but the main goal was to get involved with something tangible, even if it means developing an app that lets you hit on the girl you're sitting next to.

include pension funds, universities, and philanthropic organizations and individuals. If we are successful investors, these organizations benefit as we increase the funds they have available to make a positive impact. While this is very important, it is difficult to feel a personal connection and achieve fulfillment from these tangential rewards.

One day, I hope to find myself in an opportunity where I am not only challenged personally and intellectually (as I am in my current role), but also find a sense of fulfillment through making a tangible impact. Having moved to San Francisco over a year ago, I have gained great appreciation for the amazing things some of my peers have been able to do in technology and other industries. The products and ideas they work with have the ability to impact thousands (and sometimes millions) of people. I want to be part of a similar environment—one that is built on creativity and idea generation to power an organization and its products. Based on what I have read and learned, Stanford provides a fantastic platform for launching a career in such an environment.

Stanford's Graduate School of Business is the only graduate program that I am applying to. I am not foolish enough to think that gaining admittance to such a prestigious institution is a high-probability event, but I consider GSB to be the only program for which the rewards of attending clearly outweigh the opportunity costs. Beyond its incredible academic reputation, I find Stanford's great location and beautiful campus very appealing. I recently attended the Stanford vs. Arizona State football game and had an awesome experience cheering Stanford to victory. Although it was difficult leaving my friends on the east coast, I now ...ving in Northern California and I am in no rush to move back east!

GSB's location, world-class academic reputation, and the faculty's wealth of experience make selecting a top choice surprisingly simple. Stanford's programs in management and entrepreneurship will help me gain the skills I need to help grow an organization, and hopefully one day build one from scratch. Most importantly, it will allow me to enter a fulfilling career where I am making an impact.

WRITER'S WORDS OF WISDOM

I'm a believer that your resume and application get you "in the door," but an important contributor to success is seeming like a normal, down-to-Earth individual during your admissions interview. You want to show excitement about the opportunity without appearing overzealous.

PART
III

MEDICINE/ NURSING/ HEALTH

CHAPTER

26

Rush Medical College

"Give me 10. If you don't do it now, you'll regret it!" yells the coxswain of our Varsity 8 as we stroke through the 1,300 meter mark. Our opponent's boat is 4 seats up in the homestretch, with 700 meters to go. The lactic acid has been building up in my arms, and my leg muscles are searing at this pace. My mind is focused on the relentless beat of the coxswain and the elemental drive to succeed. This is the culmination of countless hours of predawn training virtually every day from the August heat to the February freeze. In this moment, 5 1/2 minutes seems like a lifetime. But I've made a commitment to my team and myself to leave nothing behind. As my oar bends against the rushing water for the last time in that race, I know that my teammates and I have pulled every ounce of energy out of our bodies and left it all floating somewhere in the rippling Potomac.

Even before coxswains and racing shells, it was always athletics that sparked my interest in the medical field. Football and wrestling had provided me with the firsthand opportunity to learn about bone grafts, broken tibias and ankles, pulled muscles and infections. My countless hours spent with doctors, medical personnel, and trainers provided me with a front row seat to my very own "before and after" commercial. I was fascinated by their knowledge and ability to reconstitute my damaged body. In the wake of my own orthopedic knee surgery, I experienced how a prolonged lack of physical health could affect a person's psyche as well as performance.

Wanting to learn more about how treatment of a part could better the whole person, I began shadowing Dr. Bob Patek from the Illinois Bone and Joint Institute. From witnessing the very human aspect of one-on-one clinical work, to observing in the operating room a hamstring being spliced and manipulated to function as an ACL, I was able to see the entire process that I had previously experienced as a patient, but now through a new, clinical angle. In the time spent with Dr. Patek and his patients, I constantly saw how a caring physician could soothe what was once a worried patient, putting her at ease even when discussing the prospect of something as distressing as a double knee replacement. It was these experiences that turned my interest in medical processes into a desire to be a care provider like Dr. Patek.

At this point, medicine began to weave its way into different and unexpected areas of my life. Seeking new angles for my own healing, I began to explore oriental treatment techniques, like acupuncture, which piqued my interest in Chinese culture and inspired me to begin my study of the Chinese language. The difficulties that came with my time-intensive interest in Chinese taught me that I could never study or work hard enough at something that was important to me. Even after 3 years of language classes, I will be going to China for the second time this summer to improve my speaking skills and support my interest in Chinese medicine. While the steady pressure of my rigorous academic and year-round crew schedules have often tried my dedication, I've learned to become more

WRITER'S WORDS OF WISDOM

You must convince the admissions committee that you've convinced *yourself* this is undoubtedly the career you want. This can be done via having diverse experiences within the field of medicine (or whichever field it is) as well as showing that you've tried other fields (previous careers) and still landed on medicine. Being well-rounded is generally a good thing, but not if it is to the point of making them question your ability to be dedicated to one field. Having experiences where you've persevered in times of trial is crucial, because you will have those experiences within medical school and they need to know you can handle it.

organized and efficient. I know that my physically and mentally arduous lifestyle will aptly prepare me for the demands of a medical vocation.

Athletics has pulled me into the world of medicine, so it seems natural that it should be the avenue through which I could influence the health of my community. While I have worked as a "dark room" assistant to radiologists at the Washington Hospital Center, I prefer the person-to-person nature of my community service because it makes the most of my socially engaging personality, honed as the youngest boy in a family of seven. I'm a member of Grassroot Hoyas, an organization established and run by student-athletes that uses the role model status of college athletes as a platform from which to spread HIV/AIDS awareness and prevention in the DC area. I have come to identify myself so strongly with this program because it not only seeks to educate at-risk youth living in my greater community, but also provides me with an opportunity to use my athletic background as a vehicle to affect this endemic health issue through social change. In a city that has 11 times the national average of people living with HIV, it seems amazing that many of the adolescents here have been raised in an environment that doesn't acknowledge the present danger posed by HIV/AIDS. Though the goal of these 10-week programs is to teach the children life skills that will help them make healthy decisions, I feel as though I am benefiting just as much from my time spent with these young students.

Though I may agree with these teens about who is the best hip-hop artist, socioeconomic differences between their background and mine are huge. Their very different pressures and experiences are ones that I had never been exposed to at that age. Teaching and playing with these kids has helped me mature as a person whose future plans are in the medical field. It has put my goals in medicine into perspective, reminding me that medicine can take form through social change and caring, personal inter-actions, as I had first seen with Dr. Patek. Though the gains this program has made in its pilot year are nothing less than impressive, Grassroot Hoyas lies entirely in the hands of student-athletes and it mandates our complete dedication to ensure its expansion and success in the coming years.

BRINGING IT HOME

The author ties together how these past experiences have led him to pursue a career in medicine and what he hopes to achieve by attending medical school within this strong conclusion.

From early mornings that start at 6 a.m. on the cold and torrent Potomac, to days spent volunteering in inner-city DC, to evenings that end with me studying a culture on the other side of the world, I have found that the multifaceted groundwork I have laid helps propel me to achieve more. And as the coxswain in my head yells when I tire, I know that if I don't put in the consistent dedication needed to accomplish my goals, I'm going to regret it.

CHAPTER

27

Vanderbilt University School of Medicine

In 1985, my abuela Marta Pérez, for whom I am named, died from complications resulting from pneumonia. She was born in Havana, Cuba, and when Castro's regime took over, she and my abuelo decided to flee the country. They left a comfortable upper middle class life for the freedom of the United States. When they arrived in America, universities would not recognize my grandmother's Ph.D. She went back to school and earned two master's degrees and a Ph.D. while raising six children. My abuela said that the Cuban communist regime could take material things from her, but could never take her education. Her strong emphasis on education was accompanied by a desire to enrich the lives of others, which is why she taught as a university professor. I have spent many moments in my life wondering what my abuela was like and many members of my family have told me she would be very proud of me for my hard work and dedication. Her life, values, and early death help explain why I have chosen to participate in research and to become a doctor.

Research can use scholarship to improve the lives of others. I work as a research assistant in

CRAFTING THE INTRODUCTION

This essay has a powerful introduction that provides insight into the applicant's motivation for pursuing a medical degree.

the Children's Digital Media Center at Georgetown University. I study the effects of media on children in a physical health, educational, and developmental context. I have worked on a study examining if the Wii gaming system can be used as an exercise tool for low-income middle and high school students, a population in which obesity is prevalent. I also explore how infants can learn how to perform a cognitive motor task from either a live or screen demonstration. Since children have no ability to learn from screen media if they do not actually watch it, I am also assisting on a study to understand if infants attend better to high- or low-paced video vignettes. Currently, I am preparing to write my Honors Thesis on an original research endeavor dealing with the effects of media on children.

Participating in the research process has informed my decision to pursue a career in medicine. Conducting research has taught me how to interact with participants in an informative, ethical, and caring manner while preserving their confidentiality. I think the researcher-participant relationship has many similarities to the doctor-patient relationship and these lessons will help me to be a good physician. Once data and results have been collected and published, the researcher moves on to a new study. However I have found that my greater passion lies in applying the discoveries of research to the community. Doctors have the unique ability to use education, dedication, and research performed by others in the medical and academic community toward the goal of extending and bettering the lives of individuals. While research has allowed me to develop skills to be a good physician, it has also helped me decide with certainty that my future lies in medicine.

As an ocean rescue lifeguard for three summers in Neptune Beach, FL, I was able to develop many skills that will help me to be a great doctor. Acute observational skills are required to watch for dangerous situations and prevent beachgoers from entering into them. In the event of emergencies, which were not

WRITER'S WORDS OF WISDOM

It's hard to anticipate what admissions people are looking for from an undergraduate perspective, but after being in medical school a few years you really gain perspective on what makes a good doctor.

uncommon, I was able to think quickly and use emergency medical techniques I had learned as a First Responder to make important decisions under high-pressure situations. Whether a swimmer had been rescued from a riptide, broken a wrist, or received a jellyfish sting, patient care was of the utmost importance. In many cases, the patients were scared or in shock and helping them to calm down, understand the problem, and to determine the best choice of treatment helped me learn important patient care skills. Finally, as a lifeguard on duty on a busy beach, I acted as responsible for the lives of the swimmers and people on the beach. In these ways, my extensive experience as a lifeguard exposed me to important decision making under pressure and working as a first responder gave me insight to patient care.

At Georgetown University, I have improved my leadership skills through my involvement in New Student Orientation and Blue and Gray Society. These leadership experiences are meaningful to me because I believe getting to know peers and faculty and being an active member of the campus community are very important parts of student life. When I become a doctor, I do not plan to limit my career to the inside of a hospital or office but instead to integrate myself into my community through leadership. I have already begun to do this in my home community of Jacksonville, FL, through the Leadership Jacksonville organization. Participating in LJ programs for high school and college students, I have seen the impact that concerned citizens have on their community. Most importantly, these experiences have shown me some of the areas in my community that need the most help and where I could make an impact as a doctor

> **DRAFTING PERSONAL COMMENTS ESSAYS FOR MEDICAL SCHOOL**
>
> The mechanics: The Personal Comments essay is sent to all of the medical schools to which you apply within the AMCAS system, and it should be approximately one page in length (5,300 characters).
>
> The content: The Personal Comments essay should convey the reason(s) why you are interested in pursuing medical school. Before sitting down to write the essay, it would be beneficial to brainstorm ideas about motivations and reflections that are unique to you and about how to most effectively use these concepts to convey your commitment to the field.

such as prenatal care for poor mothers, preventative treatment for heart disease and breast cancer, and education about fitness and nutrition to fight obesity. These leadership and educational experiences have helped confirm my decision to be a physician and given me insight into possible specialties to pursue.

28

University of Southern California
Division of Biokinesiology & Physical Therapy

Describe your decision making process in choosing physical therapy as a career choice versus other health care careers.

As I stepped into the clinic, the sobering sight of the scarred, stitched, and bandaged residual limbs of soldiers elicited a sorrowful lump in my throat. A second later, a soldier sprinted by me on the indoor track, precariously rounding the curves and regaining control of his stride with surprising deftness in his two "Cheetah Blade" prosthetic feet. Throughout the bustling clinic, physical therapists and doc-

AVOIDING TEMPTATION

Note the very specific nature of this prompt. Writers may be tempted to begin addressing this prompt with "I want to be a physical therapist because . . ." As you read this essay, focus on how the author crafts a personal statement that is sincere and well-written, completely avoiding clichés or lackluster language.

tors looked on with pride, and fellow soldiers and patients cheered with aspiring admiration. The knot of unwanted pity in my throat vanished in a gasp of excitement.

These soldiers did not seek pity. Humbly and bravely, they sought support while striving to regain the highest degree of functional independence possible. For the next few weeks at the Amputee Clinic of the Military Advanced Training Center (MATC) at Walter Reed National Military Medical Center, I witnessed and partook in such support.

The patients and physical therapists in the MATC invigorated me daily, stoking a passion to pursue a career in which I could empower patients to recover. Although only a small demographic within the patient population, the soldiers at Walter Reed in conjunction with their physical therapists highlighted both the importance of a strong therapist-patient relationship and a creative holistic approach to problem solving, as well as the appeal of the altruistic drive behind physical therapy.

The unique and multifaceted medical conditions of these soldiers require several months, potentially years, of treatment. During those months, the physical therapist invests time and energy into developing a relationship with the patient in order to understand better the patient's needs and goals. My experience in the MATC taught me how a therapist plays a continuous role throughout most of the healing process, as opposed to merely prescribing a quick-fix treatment.

This fall, as a Physical Education teacher in a school for children with special needs, I have been forming just such relationships with children on the autism spectrum. As with PT patients, these children experience a complex combination of conditions including self-regulation challenges in executive functioning, proprioception, and social anxiety. Additionally, in concert with the goals of physical therapy, the mission of our unique school involves providing these children with tools to function healthily and relatively independently in daily personal and social life.

As in grade school academia, the development of an authentic personal relationship between the therapist and the person seeking therapy underscores not only the altruistic nature of PT in which the therapist strives to help those in need, but also the inventive problem solving involved in treating a PT patient. Determining how most effectively to treat a patient, or to instruct a child on the autism spectrum, requires a comprehensive understanding of the individual's past experiences, his or her current physical, mental, and emotional conditions, and his or her aspirations for the future.

As I spend time with my students, I channel the discipline and attention to detail that I developed while studying undergraduate physics to scrutinize student reactions and interactions in order to tailor my lesson plans to the students' needs. From eye movements and focus when throwing and catching a football, to reactions after missing a free throw, each action and response informs me as to how I can better serve the individual students and the class as a whole.

The physical therapists at Walter Reed introduced me to this holistic approach to treating individuals whose conditions span several medical fields. In addition to time in the Amputee Clinic, I witnessed and assisted with biomedical-PT research that aims to develop and to improve equipment and treatment methods. In the Center for Performance and Clinical Research, organizing data for a study on the effects of prosthetic use on metabolic rate during physical activity and observing appointments of patients who use the Computer Animated Research Environment (CAREN) exposed me to the breadth of innovation in this field of medicine.

The therapists' flexibility, creativity, and collaboration fueled by a genuine desire to serve the wounded soldiers continue to inspire me as I address the daily challenges of children with unique neurological, emotional, and physical needs in hopes of applying a similar work ethic as a physical therapist.

WRITER'S WORDS OF WISDOM

During the application process, invest your time, effort, and money learning about and applying to the handful of schools that you really want to attend, as opposed to spending, and potentially wasting, your time, effort, and money applying to 15 schools, 10 of which you only sort of like.

CHAPTER 29

Yale School of Public Health

When I began teaching English in a rural Panamanian village after my first year of college, I expected to learn about teaching methods and educational disparities. Instead, I learned that education can be a luxury for so many people in light of daily struggles with illness, malnutrition, and lack of access to health care. Most of the town, including my host family, did not have running water or reliable electricity. Its health clinic, desperately short-staffed and difficult to reach by road, had all but shut its doors. Malnourishment kept many of my students from staying alert in class. This experience profoundly impacted my evolving interests and ambitions and opened my eyes to the potential to have a positive impact on the lives of others through public health.

I have always been fascinated by cultural difference, and as I started college I was immediately drawn to anthropology. My experiences in Panama added a new dimension to my interests, teaching me that health and culture are inextricably bound. Combating disease effectively requires more than medical science; the key to successful health interventions resides at the intersection of the social, cultural, biological, economic, political, and environmental forces that shape populations.

Throughout college, I actively explored the interests sparked by my summer in Panama. Beyond coursework in anthropology, sociology, international health, human rights, and women's studies, I worked in a diverse array of settings throughout Washington, DC, and Brazil. As I learned about the health issues confronting sex workers, injection drug users, and HIV patients without access to care, I developed a strong interest in sexual and reproductive health issues that impact vulnerable populations in the United States and globally. I am committed to increasing access to services for these populations and to reducing the stigma around many of the issues they face. My undergraduate academic experience culminated in two senior theses: one exploring political activism among HIV-positive women in the United States and the other assessing the role of civil society in the development of Brazilian HIV treatment policies.

Over the past 6 years, I have worked with Helping Individual Prostitutes Survive (HIPS), a nonprofit organization that provides harm reduction services to sex workers and injection drug users in Washington, DC. When I started at HIPS during my first year of college, I was trained as an outreach volunteer, spending two nights each month driving throughout the city distributing condoms, providing safer-sex counseling, and helping to administer a needle-exchange program. Through my 6 years there, I have gained valuable experience discussing health issues with a diverse array of people and become a team leader for groups of outreach volunteers and an HIV counselor and tester.

Instead of studying abroad during my third year, I took a one-semester leave of absence to volunteer full-time with CAMTRA, a community-based organization in Rio de Janeiro, Brazil. During my time at CAMTRA, I supported CAMTRA's outreach programs that worked to increase access to information about sexual health and domestic violence, and I helped to facilitate discussion forums for girls in secondary schools about women's health and rights issues. As the only foreigner working with this organization, my volunteer work at CAMTRA provided me with a valuable cultural immersion experience. Over my final year at Georgetown, I also completed an internship at the Women's Collective, which advocates and provides services for HIV-positive women. I spent the year working with a group of HIV-positive women on efforts to increase the voice of their community in influencing national HIV policies.

My current position at the Office of the U.S. Global AIDS Coordinator has enabled me to contribute to the development of international health policy. Through my work, I have seen the vital role that public health analysis and research play in the well-being of people and communities throughout the world.

From the interpersonal to the international, my volunteer, academic, and professional experiences have given me several perspectives into the interactions between health and society, and have affirmed my desire to pursue a career in public health. Yale University's Masters of Public Health in Social and Behavioral Sciences would be an ideal setting to explore my passion for public health and transform it into work that meaningfully touches the lives of other people. Yale's commitment to practical applications of public health principles and research will give me the skills I need to follow this career path.

WRITER'S WORDS OF WISDOM

I talked to a few admissions folks about resume length, and they encouraged me to send everything, even if it seemed long.

I am particularly drawn to Yale because of its small program, where I will have the opportunity to work closely with outstanding faculty members, and because of the opportunity to conduct community-based public health research and practice in collaboration organizations like the Center for Interdisciplinary Research on AIDS and the Connecticut Women's Health Project.

I am especially drawn to the concentration in Global Health. This program's interdisciplinary approach to health resonates deeply with my academic and practical experiences, drawing together economic, political, cultural, historical, and social issues related to risk for disease, violence, and access to healthcare services. Following graduation, I plan to work with marginalized populations to develop rights-based programs and conduct operational research with the goal of helping these communities improve their health status through creative and evidence-based problem-solving. The values of the Yale School of Public Health mirror my desires to address health disparities in vulnerable populations, promote a human rights-based approach to health, and learn from the populations that I work to serve.

CHAPTER

30

George Washington University

School of Public Health and Health Services

Describe the experiences that have shaped your interest in public health.

As a non-pre-med, biology major I have always had my sights set on aspects of science that extend beyond purely medicine. I have used my interest in science as a means to learn about its connections to everyday life, including the role that research plays in the public health arena. Throughout my time at Georgetown I have taken classes that combine scientific processes with their counterparts in public policy. My experiences in classes such as Virology and Parasitology have blended the detail necessary to understand these microorganisms with their impact on public health. By studying the discovery, transmission, and prevention of individual parasites and viruses, I have found myself seeking knowledge in public health practices as well as the molecular arena I had previously been familiar with.

CRAFTING THE SHORT ANSWER

As if it wasn't already difficult enough to condense graduate school aspirations into 2 pages, try doing it in 200 words. With little room for anecdotes and personal touches, the short answer requires the author to be concise, which this essay's author executes expertly.

To satisfy my growing desire for knowledge in these two fields I began attending conferences hosted by the Biology of Global Health department at Georgetown and enrolled in an International Health course on Global Patterns of Disease. This most recent course has combined epidemiological processes with a strong background in the public health policies and practices instituted by the WHO, CDC, PAHO, and other international organizations. My professor's extensive knowledge and broad range of experiences in the field have served as a resource for me to learn about the opportunities available for individuals in public health. I think that George Washington University's program is a perfect blend of my continued interest in microbiology and my blossoming interest in public health.

How do you propose to use your training and education from GW once you graduate?

The program offered by George Washington University not only combines two areas of study that I am extremely interested in, but it also offers an incredible location for continued work and experiences in the field. I am eager to utilize the resources that the nation's capital has to offer, especially given its growing demand for individuals that are trained in microbiology and biochemical threat agents.

Upon graduating I would be interested in working for a governmental agency such as the Federal Bureau of Investigation, National Institute of Health, or the Department of Health and Human Services. After gaining valuable hands-on experiences through working with one of these organizations, I would like to return to school and obtain my Ph.D. Through my work with the Howard Hughes Teaching Institute I have gained valuable tools in pedagogical practice, which I hope to ultimately utilize by returning to teach at an institute of higher education. I would hope to utilize the knowledge gained from my experiences in the public health arena to inform and inspire a new generation of individuals to continue the work required by such a crucial field.

WRITER'S WORDS OF WISDOM

Once you're there, don't be afraid to take electives outside of your program. Just because it's grad school and it's supposed to be super specialized doesn't mean you still can't find something new to be interested in and excited about.

CHAPTER
31

Northeastern University
Bouvé College of Health Sciences

Future of nursing and purpose for applying for graduate study:

I have been privileged to work in a profession that satisfies me, challenges me, and teaches me something new every day. I sincerely love my work and the opportunity I get to make a difference in the lives of patients, their family members, and my coworkers. The field of nursing affords me the opportunity to incorporate my interest in the intricacies of the human body with my passion to care for people in their time of vulnerability. As vital members of the health care team, nurses are in close contact with patients and therefore have the unique opportunity to positively influence the outcomes of a patient's hospital course. The future holds incredible opportunities in the field of nursing as the health care situation necessitates that it expand to meet the growing demand for high-quality medical care.

I am pursuing a graduate degree from Northeastern University because I am a person who constantly looks for new challenges and opportunities to learn and gain knowledge. I want to grow and expand in the nursing profession. I believe that in pursuing a master's degree in nurse anesthesia, I can become a frontline person in the care of patients in one of their most vulnerable states—under anesthesia—and I have chosen Northeastern University for its strong curriculum and opportunities through its various clinical sites.

Choice of specialty and role:

My choice to pursue a degree in nurse anesthesia comes from my love of the intensity of the critical care setting. I have spent my nursing career in a neuro ICU and a surgical trauma burn ICU where I thrive on the high intensity and energy. Working in a critical care setting requires the ability to "think on one's feet," utilizing critical thinking skills to apply evidence-based principles, often within split seconds when a crisis evolves. I have been praised by preceptors and supervisors for my ability to adapt to situations and to problem solve. I am often the "go-to" person when assignments are made for the most complicated patients on the unit.

I have had the opportunity to shadow multiple nurse anesthetists in the hospital. I have been amazed at the vast amount of knowledge a CRNA must have to be able to care for the patient and manage their anesthesia. As the person who is responsible for monitoring the anesthetized patient, the CRNA needs to be

WRITER'S WORDS OF WISDOM

Try your best to do something that stands out. Whether it be in your essay, resume, interview, or even down to writing hand-written notes. Anyone who asks for my best piece of advice on getting into grad school or getting a job is you can never underestimate the power of a hand-written note. People are all about e-mailing, etc. these days, but I think it shows that you are very interested in the position and are willing to take the time to express that. Try to remember some little personal thing/connection you had with each person you meet, whether they also like the beach, or their son or daughter plays lacrosse, something personal to show that you remember and care, and put a one-liner in your note about that.

able to critically think and quickly intervene. The CRNA also has the unique opportunity to educate and comfort patients before and after surgery. This is a part of the nursing profession that I value highly as I continuously seek opportunities to incorporate support and education into my care. Nurse anesthesia is a needed and growing field, which I hope to use my knowledge and skills to advance even further.

Future plans:

My immediate future plans are to gain a master's degree in nurse anesthesia from Northeastern University and upon graduation to gain experience and knowledge working as a CRNA, continuing to care for critically ill patients. My long-term goal is to take my desire to serve and my knowledge in nurse anesthesia to an underprivileged area in the world to help those who may not have the healthcare resources they desperately need. As a teen, and then again as a nursing student, I spent time volunteering in Africa, and I was overwhelmed by the need for medical care and resources. I had the opportunity to assist in medical clinics providing basic health measures like hygiene education and de-worming treatments. I would love to partner with a healthcare team to bring life-saving surgeries to a region where medical services are so rare. I am confident a master's degree from Northeastern University would help me achieve this dream.

ORGANIZING YOUR THOUGHTS

The author presents a strong example of how to organize the body of the essay. You may want to start your essay by using these kinds of headers so that you capture the information you want to include without worrying about transitions. Then, you can either decide to leave the headers or take them out, based on your personal preference.

CHAPTER
32

Georgetown University School of Medicine
Department of Microbiology and Immunology

From the time I was in fourth grade until I entered college, my goal was to become an orthopedic surgeon. I have always been a type-A student that had everything planned out; I knew exactly where my life was headed. Then I came to Georgetown University. Freshman year started on a pre-med path, but I began to question whether it was the right fit. Increasingly, I exposed myself to a wider variety of subjects and realized what a wealth of opportunities college offered. Although science remained a priority, I discovered government classes piqued my interest as well. When the Biology Department began offering the Biology of Global Health major my sophomore year, I embraced it as the perfect opportunity to combine both of my passions: basic science and international health. I was mostly intrigued by the magnitude of impact disease has on a global spectrum and how it is responsible for intertwining cul-

AVOIDING OVERUSING "I"

If you take a look at the above paragraph, you will note how the author does not fall into the trap of beginning every sentence with the word "I." Because admissions essays are highly personal, it can be easy to fall into the habit of using the word "I": "I want to attend this program because . . . I gained experience in the field with . . . etc." The author excels at using an assortment of prepositional phrases and sentence subjects to form an essay that avoids repetition and flows naturally.

tures. This process brought the realization that I wanted to focus increasingly on policy in combination with biology following graduation.

Subsequent work experience with the Facilities, Security, and Emergency Management department at the Department of Education underlined my increasing interest in emergency management and homeland security. Through my work I witnessed the field's constant fluidity as well as need for a complementary blend of creative thinking and policy implementation to function efficiently. This field incorporated many of my interests, from the science of biological and nuclear weapons to international relations. As a team member, I addressed many situations including security threats and swine flu precautions. My time and experience with these two fields, in addition to hands-on crisis preparation and management, led me to the realization I wanted to enter the homeland security field.

Through my employment after graduation for the Cystic Fibrosis Foundation, I have seen firsthand how scientific evidence can be used to help create and influence policy and procedures at a nonprofit organization. As part of the Operations Department, I grew to understand the internal process of the organization, from raising money for research and scientific trials, pharmaceutical transactions, public policy, as well as interaction with grant providers and the government. Through my work experience, I realize I have an affinity for the application part of the process. My goal is to be a part of formulating and implementing policies that will benefit the public and country as a whole, specifically in the homeland security field.

After completing my graduate degree, my long-term goal is to pursue a career in the government or as a government contractor. I desire to play a role in formulating the best policies and procedures that will help, protect, and serve the homeland security of the United States. I believe this is a very demanding, evolving, and unique field that will challenge me to excel and increase my knowledge on an ongoing basis. In order to accomplish this, I must acquire the knowledge relevant to the application of these policies. Having attended Georgetown University for undergraduate school, I know what a tremendous academic education it provides for the whole person as well as the numerous opportunities available inside and outside of the classroom. With my science background, firsthand experiences at a nonprofit organization, and strong drive to succeed, I am confident I would offer positive contributions in return to the Biohazardous Threat Agents and Emerging Infectious Diseases program at Georgetown University.

WRITER'S WORDS OF WISDOM

Before jumping right into a graduate program, I would recommend taking a year or two to work first. You learn a lot of practical life lessons that professors don't cover in classes and it gives you a chance to figure out what you really want to go back to school for—you learn a lot once you first start working and this may influence your decision. Then, when you are applying, this gives you a different perspective than many applicants and helps you stand out.

University of North Carolina at Chapel Hill

Gillings School of Global Public Health

Quite frankly, I get it. I understand the pressure. I understand the need for your body to move both gracefully and fiercely across the stage. I have received the praise, I've heard the criticisms, and I've both struggled with and acknowledged my flaws. In so many ways, I get it.

When I enrolled at a Cecchiti ballet studio at age 4, I never imagined how hard I would fall in love with dance. Over the next 14 years, my passion evolved gracefully, as if each double pirouette and pas de bourrée unfolded a different dimension of my love for ballet. The main reason that I fell so hard for dance was my studio; it empowered me to be as serious about the art form as I pleased. Though I was encouraged to focus, stretch, and improve, I was never expected to transform my life or body for dance.

Over time, as I improved and started attending regional and national dance conventions and performances, I discovered that many young girls at other studios were not granted the same liberties. I saw how girls who faced rigorous demands consequently demanded too much from their own bodies. Negative body image and eating disorders flourished around me, and I could sympathize with their frustrations. While I was thankfully among the pack that was, for the most part, able to receive and ignore harsh dance and body criticisms, I watched so many friends and fellow dancers struggle. I became fascinated that we could all wear the same leotards, the same shoes, and move and stretch to the exact same exercises every evening . . . and react so differently.

Over the next 10 years, I recognized two very important things. First, the demands on the ballet community are extreme, and the goals placed before these girls can often not be reached. Second, these girls and boys who struggle with eating disorders do not just need therapists to counsel them; they need compassionate professionals in every field who will promote positive body image and self-confidence.

For so many years, I was tunnel-visioned toward a career as a clinical psychologist so I could be a therapist for these dancers. I rarely considered any other options. Then, when completing my clinical hours during my Masters in Health Psychology at the University of St Andrews, I discovered a fascinating intersection of psychology and physical health. The health psychologists in Scotland spent hours talking to individuals recently diagnosed with diabetes who were struggling with both the reality of the diagnosis and the new lifestyle required to control their symptoms. They advised other patients with heart disease who had no idea how to reduce their cholesterol and develop a healthier lifestyle. The health psychologists equally valued the physical and mental health of each patient, and they spent time nurturing both dimensions.

Then, when I accepted a position as a research assistant at a center focusing on eating disorders, I saw how my passion for psychology, my lifelong interest in eating disorder research, and the balance of physical and mental health converged on one field: nutrition. Dietitians

FORGING YOUR OWN PATH

The strength of this essay lies in the author's ability to describe her journey to identify her professional interests and discover the intersection of her passions, even when it diverged from her original goals.

help patients with eating disorders overcome their deep fear of change. They value the physical health of each patient by devising individual meal plans and manageable goals while remaining sympathetic of their fear of weight gain and guilt. Just like the health psychologists in Scotland, these dietitians contribute to the physical and mental health of each patient, and I found their passion to be incredibly inspiring.

The Masters in Public Health/Registered Dietitian program at UNC is specifically designed to help its students explore and appreciate all dimensions of health. Unlike so many registered dietitian programs, the UNC curriculum is focused on creating balanced practitioners; students are exposed to scientific, psychological, and social aspects of health. I want to attend a program that will expose me to every area, challenging me to evolve into an effective member of the public and private health sectors. The MPH/RD program at UNC provides this unique opportunity.

Additionally, though I am confident in my passion for eating disorders, I am committed to remaining open-minded about my career and specialties. My career path has already evolved a number of different times, drawing me toward specific classes, certain internships, and different professional relationships with professors and postdoctoral students. During the MPH/RD program, I will take classes on maternal/child health, nutrition for the elderly, and nutritional epidemiology. I will journey with my UNC classmates to Washington, DC, to be part of health's political movement. I will work each summer in public health and clinical settings. This specific program at UNC will allow my passion for public health and nutrition to continue to evolve during every course and summer experience.

Additionally, having spent the past 2 years as a research intern and then research assistant/coordinator, I am passionate about continuing to help with ongoing eating disorder research projects. I recognize the need for informed dietitians to contribute ideas to new and continuing research studies, and I would love to begin helping in this capacity.

When I complete my degree, I am excited to become a dietitian who continues working with ballet dancers and other athletes to help them to both strengthen their bodies and maintain a healthy, realistic lifestyle. I

WRITER'S WORDS OF WISDOM

When you are applying to undergrad, prospective schools often focus on grades, SAT scores, and other important "numbers" that will help them determine whether or not you are competitive for their program. Now, as you apply to grad school, they are really focusing on the total package. They want to know more about where you have been, what you have learned, and what experiences you have had. Although "the numbers" will always be important to some degree, focus on stressing how you are special and what unique experiences you can contribute to the classroom. Grad schools want to know how you are different, not how perfect you can score on a test. In other words, set yourself apart.

will work with my clients to develop meal plans, to explain basic nutrition, and to provide valuable advice for change. Simultaneously, I will always strive to convey a message of body acceptance and self-love. Why? These impressionable young boys and girls need someone who equally values physical and mental health. They also need someone who understands the pressure . . . and in so many ways, I get it.

Georgetown University
School of Nursing & Health Studies

Cura Personalis, care for the whole person, will forever be embedded in my nursing practices, every day, with every patient. Nursing is both innate abilities and learned knowledge. As an undergraduate, Georgetown University channeled my passion for healthcare and laid the foundation to think critically as a nurse. When I began my career as a new graduate, I realized I was exceptionally well prepared and appreciated how amazing my nursing curriculum was. In hindsight, attending Georgetown's School of Nursing & Health Studies was the best decision I ever made. I am proud to be a Hoya, RN.

I want to be a Family Nurse Practitioner, and I look forward to expanding my knowledge, nursing abilities, and scope of practice to serve others: "Men and Women for others." As an RN I demonstrate the characteristics needed to be a successful APRN. Each night I begin my shift

WRITER'S WORDS OF WISDOM

Make your passion come alive for the reader.

with contagious energy and optimism. Before clocking out each morning, I ask my coworkers if I can help them with anything. I am known by the L&D team for wanting the challenging patient assignments: drug addicts, teenagers, the homeless, prostitutes, "frequent flyers." I proceed without judgment, and I proudly advocate for their fair and thorough care. I am an efficient communicator. As a kid on the soccer field, I was always very verbal and communicated with my teammates. "Pass to midfield . . . I'm open . . . We need more defense . . . You take the shot . . . I need help . . ." I find myself in a similar position as part of our "Special Deliveries" team. I am neither timid nor boastful; I am not afraid to delegate, collaborate, prioritize, or strategize. Following one of my most complex and tragic emergencies in labor and delivery, resulting in an imminent maternal death, my coworker said, "Now, Liz is someone you want when your ship is sinking."

My range of clinical experiences and interests motivates me every day to work toward my dream of opening a clinic. I am drawn toward specialties of public health, adolescents, mental health, dermatology, international health, and women's health. I am intrigued by vulnerable patient populations and aspire to work in communities to make a difference. "Be the change you want to see in the world." I consider Gandhi's words as my own mantra to live by. Working with migrant families, caring for foster children, providing care at Planned Parenthood, and advocating and caring for victims of domestic abuse, sexual violence, or the homeless are just the beginning of how I hope to make an impact as an FNP.

Adolescents are the vulnerable population I would like to dedicate my career to and establish a practice with care catered toward the young adult. The age-specific care for teens and young adults is often overlooked and is lacking. These patients are stranded between levels of health care: pediatric versus adult practices. I will become a primary care provider to help these teens grow into healthy adults, focusing on health promotion and disease prevention.

WRITER'S WORDS OF WISDOM

Be proud of the person you are and the person you wish to become.

My plan is to create a primary care center for teens and young adults, ages 13 to 23, offering primary and preventive care, gynecology, mental health, nutrition, and dermatology. There would also be an immunization promotion office, targeting patients traveling abroad, precollege vaccines, or learning more about the benefits of Gardasil. Realistic access to healthcare is crucial in providing care for vulnerable populations. Creating a nonjudgmental environment helps minimize the patient's fears of seeking medical attention, and enables practitioners to create a trusting relationship with the patient. Personally, as a teenager my mom switched pediatric offices multiple times because of difficulty getting appointments or being disappointed in the care provided as my sister and I got older. I delayed going to the gynecologist due to fear of asking my parents to take me. I also struggled with mental health conditions, which ultimately warranted attention years earlier because I didn't know who to go to or what to do, nor did I know if those emotions and behaviors were just normal. In my proposed clinic, young girls would be getting the gynecologic care and knowledge they need, instead of avoiding the health responsibilities. This age group especially needs access to counseling and behavioral health, probably more than any other patient population. I strongly believe that health is composed of the mind, body, and spirit, and an imbalance hinders overall health.

WRITER'S WORDS OF WISDOM

Try using fewer words to explain yourself and the statements become bolder.

I am searching for the right graduate program that continues to fuel my passion. Nursing@Georgetown and I are a perfect match. I am dedicated to our profession, and I know this MSN program will prepare me for my career endeavors. I would be overjoyed to continue my graduate studies at Georgetown University. I look forward to reaching my curriculum goals: mastering assessment; identifying diagnoses; providing patient education; collaborating with practitioners; and conducting scholarly research. As I review the "Student Spotlights" on the program's website, I see dreamers, students, and nurses just like myself. Their motivation and passions are tangible. The environment makes a significant difference in any experience, especially school. I

STAYING POSITIVE

The positive tone of this essay allows readers to see that the author is passionate about her career and that she is excited about taking the next step in education to achieve her goals. Instead of complaining about the program in which she had previously enrolled, the author takes the opportunity to highlight a favorable characteristic of the university to which she is applying.

recognized this after completing three semesters of an MSN/FNP program at Barry University in Miami, FL. I missed the enthusiasm of classmates and professors that I once felt at Georgetown as a BSN student. I want to be on a team with more individuals like myself, students who choose to learn and prosper together; students and teachers who are equally motivated, professional, and eager to take on this challenge. I desire a program where students enhance each other's learning experience, sharing our various backgrounds and specialties, as we embark on this journey together in becoming Family Nurse Practitioners.

CHAPTER
35

The Ohio State University College of Medicine

I did not enter college with the goal of becoming a physician; I entered college with the goal of becoming a lawyer, or a writer, or a businesswoman, etc. I had been surrounded by the medical profession all of my life, as both of my parents are physicians, but I continually shrugged off the curiosity I felt toward medicine. However, as a college freshman, I soon found myself eavesdropping on students who were studying human biology and was unenthused by my international relations class. Realizing I missed science classes, I decided to start taking the premedicine course work and have since developed a passionate desire to become a physician.

In the summer between my sophomore and junior years in college, I worked in an outpatient Internal Medicine Center performing research, shadowing doctors, and interacting with patients. The Center is an ambulatory care clinic that serves an impoverished community. For the first time, I was presented with the challenges that come with caring for patients who lack a permanent address and cannot afford food, let alone medical care. My interactions with these patients taught me more about the practice of medicine than any textbook ever could. For instance, when I was talking with an overweight, depressed patient with diabetes who could not afford her insulin, she declared she was not taking insulin anymore because she "Just didn't feel like it." Even though the physician and I explained the importance of taking insulin and tried to help her lose weight, this patient's condition had worsened by the end of summer. I questioned why she was not following her doctor's orders and did not initially realize that there were many complicated, underlying reasons why she refused to take her medication; it was not simply because she did not feel like it or was lazy. To this patient, providing food for her family and avoiding homelessness were higher priorities than her medical care. On top of that, her doctor told me that her depression makes her feel hopeless toward improving her health, so she does not see the point in taking insulin.

Through my interactions with this patient and others, I began to appreciate the complexity involved in caring for all patients. It is not as simple as diagnosing the problem, prescribing medication, and curing the patient. There are many factors at play when prescribing a treatment plan, and the physician has to take into account the patient's willingness to adhere to the plan when prescribing treatment. This experience taught me that each individual patient requires a personalized care plan. Along with providing effective medical care, a physician must also provide compassion and understanding to the patient so he or she can treat each patient in the most appropriate manner.

DETERMINING MOTIVATIONS

When brainstorming essay topics, consider thinking back to when you first pinpointed your interest in your chosen profession and see where this leads you, just as this author does within the Personal Comments portion of her medical school application.

The same summer, while shadowing a doctor in the hospital, he was paged to respond to a Code Blue. Racing to the patient's room, scenes from *Grey's Anatomy* and *ER* flashed through my mind, but as we entered the room, we discovered that the woman was "do not resuscitate." The situation quickly calmed and the doctor made everyone leave the room except me and a nurse. He called the woman's daughter into the room, and administered appropriate care to the patient. He calmly and kindly told the daughter that her mother only had a few minutes to live and sat her in a chair by the patient's bed. He then made me leave the room while he and the nurse stayed until the patient died.

Having physicians as parents, I knew that medicine was not the glorified version on TV, however this situation confirmed my understanding that a physician must find a balance between being scientific, compassionate, and understanding. I truly admire how the doctor handled this situation with respect, by first making the other doctors leave, then allowing the daughter to be with her mother while he stood by, quietly making sure he fulfilled his duty to the patient and gave her the appropriate care. He did what he needed to do for his patient by making her comfortable and letting her die with the dignity she had requested.

Through my summer at the outpatient Internal Medicine Center, volunteering at a hospital, and the many other opportunities I have had to shadow physicians in the NICU and ER, I have had the opportunity to interact with a variety of physicians and patients. I appreciate that the practice of medicine is challenging and understand the complexities and responsibilities that come with being a physician.

However, I am confident that I am up for the challenge.

WRITER'S WORDS OF WISDOM

Make sure you are actually interested in the practice of medicine; shadow a physician, volunteer in the hospital, interact with patients, etc., so you can at least get a taste of what the profession actually entails. Medicine is a wonderful profession, and I can't see myself doing anything else, but medical school applicants should not take the decision to apply to medical school lightly.

PART

IV

GENERAL GRADUATE STUDIES

CHAPTER
36

Middlebury College
The Bread Loaf
School of English

In my first year out of college, I moved to the big city and took a job as an Assistant Account Executive—which is to say, a peon—at a gigantic public relations firm specializing in New York City landmarks. The glamour of the company attracted me, and I'd somehow glossed over what seems to me now to be the obvious route for a graduate with a serious passion for English. So when my human resources interviewer dropped the name "Rockefeller Center" as a client, and the words "Christmas Tree Lighting," which was to be my newest, biggest event, my heart fluttered. Sitting in her office then I couldn't suppress the image: under my fur-trimmed ear-muffs, my high-tech earpiece vibrates with top secret instructions to escort an A-list celebrity from one side of the Rockefeller Center ice skating rink to the other, precisely at the moment that the 90-foot Christmas tree above us bursts into light with the glow of 100,000 megawatt Christmas bulbs. I can't explain now why that

MAKING A STRONG FIRST IMPRESSION

The author grips readers with a powerful first paragraph that is packed with detail.

vision ever seemed reasonable—let alone alluring—to me, but it did. So I took the job.

Seven months later, I was standing under that Christmas tree in the center of the Rockefeller Center ice skating rink, but the picture looked a little different. For one, I was crying—not joyful tears, but the ugly, face-reddening kind that well up despite, and because of, best efforts to remain calm. I was wearing an earpiece, and it was vibrating—with the deafening shouts of an angry boss who couldn't figure out which members of the Tokyo Foreign Press belonged behind which barricade. In that moment, I had what my friends and I refer to as an "OBOE": an Out of Body Omniscient Experience. (Draw your own conclusions from the fact that we've named this feeling, and that it includes the word "omniscient.") In my OBOE, something clicked: I was unhappy. And it didn't take a genius to trace this feeling back to its root; I had taken the wrong job, and I had known it practically from the very first day I took it. I needed to be stimulated—not by fluorescent lights and fancy names—but by a community of people who would challenge me intellectually and push me to be better.

When I finally summoned the courage to march (read: sheepishly tiptoe) into my boss's office 2 months later to deliver the news that I was leaving to pursue the career I'd actually wanted—in teaching—he said something that I'll never forget. Not a man of many words, he opened his mouth and announced, "I knew it when you started. You're such a teacher." I was floored. If this chain-smoking, cell-phone-clutching, life-long public relations devotee had known all along that I was supposed to be a teacher, how had I missed it?

His flatly delivered words, surely not meant as praise, were all the reassurance I needed that I'd made the right decision. And in the year and a half that have passed since I took a teaching fellowship position, I've never doubted it. Having had a job that I hated makes me appreciate—every single day—having one that I love. It is challenging, it is rich, it is new every day, and it is fulfilling in a way that I struggle to describe.

I teach two sections of freshmen girls, a coeducational section of sophomores, and another of seniors. The breadth of experience between class periods, even, is more diverse and enlightening than a year at my corporate job. On any given day, I spend first period dissecting blame in Capote's *In Cold Blood*, second squealing over *Pride and Prejudice's* Mr. Darcy, third period cursing Dorian Gray's mistakes in Wilde's twisted novel, and by fifth, I'm back to Mr. Darcy. I'm inspired and challenged by the students I teach, and I want, badly, to be the best version of their English teacher that I can possibly be.

This very real need is what drives me to apply to graduate school to obtain a Master of Arts Degree in English. Having taught others, I'm ready to be taught again, and to draw on my experience as an educator in order to learn in a totally new way. I consider myself fortunate that I struggle when asked about an inspirational teacher I've had. I have a laundry list. I loved English in high school, when a teacher named Scott Tucker taught me to dive in and enjoy the bliss of wrapping myself in T.S. Eliot's words, even if I didn't—and I didn't most of the time—know what they meant. I loved English in college, when Professor Libbie Rifkin dropped me squarely, and without help, into the world of twentieth-century postmodern fiction, asking me to cling to whatever shred of meaning I could find and explode it. I even loved it postcollege, when I shied away from the foreignness of applying to teaching jobs, did what my friends did, and "went corporate," spending my after-work hours poring over whichever book I'd most recently read about in the paper or borrowed from a friend. And I love it now, when I strain my ears in the English Department office to overhear the advice of a colleague to his student about topic sentences; the sheer intelligence and eloquence I'm surrounded by every day make me certain that this job is going to continue to make me better.

> **WRITER'S WORDS OF WISDOM**
>
> Talking to people who have graduated from, or are currently attending, the schools to which you're planning to apply makes a huge difference. I thought I knew exactly what I wanted out of graduate school—and where I wanted to get it from—until I had some really honest conversations with friends-of-friends and colleagues who had attended my prospective choices. What you read in a school's promotional material will never be as accurate as someone's unfiltered, firsthand experience.

Perhaps it sounds selfish, but I'm pursuing a Masters in English in order to accelerate that "bettering." I want to relearn texts I've seen before and fill in the gaps in my literary knowledge where they exist. I want to read non-Western works and take whole courses about a single text. I want to study authors and poets and literary movements with a group of people who want the same thing: to be the best version of an English teacher that they can be. I hope to teach English for as long as my professional career lasts, and as such, I can't imagine ever feeling satisfied with my knowledge of literature. Part of the allure of this job, at least for me, is in the constant, nagging thirst to know more, and to learn from those who know it—my students included. I hope that by attending graduate school, I will be able to absorb the knowledge of both my professors and my classmates, whose careers in teaching and commitment to lifelong learning will no doubt be sources of inspiration for me.

> **TYING IT ALL TOGETHER**
>
> Within her two final sentences, the author provides a conclusion that is perfectly executed in that it ties back to the introduction without repetition.

> **WRITER'S WORDS OF WISDOM**
>
> Honoring your own personality really counts. When I started my applications, I wrote about 10 drafts of personal statements, all of which sounded canned and not like me at all. But after I had gotten all of the things I thought I should say out of my system, I started writing in a voice—and telling a story—that really belonged to me. It is a personal statement, after all.

About a month ago, as I was flipping through television channels to find some ambient background noise for grading the large stack of essays in my lap, I came across the broadcast of the Rockefeller Center Christmas Tree Lighting. And in that moment, I had another OBOE: I've never been happier, and I cannot wait to continue to learn to do my job better.

CHAPTER
37

Harvard Graduate School of Education

"1 – 3 – 7 – 9 – 3 – 9 – 1 – 7." My first-grade student taught me this sequence, which can be used to find all of the prime numbers starting with 11, because the ones digits of prime numbers form a pattern. With that sequence, and with the numbers 49 and 77 as examples, I taught my first-grade student the subtlety of exceptions to rules. Numbers are orderly, predictable, and comforting. They are not irregular or erratic like a conversation, nor are they ambiguous like a smile or a glance. All the same, they are alive and meaningful to many of my students. Through 2 1/2 years of trying to take my students' perspectives, numbers have become meaningful to me too; numbers are a way I can connect with my students when they are feeling down and explain complex social nuances when they are feeling curious.

Today there are 33 students enrolled at the Auburn School in Silver Spring, MD. While that was the number of classmates I had myself as a young child, that number sounds enormous to me today. It is more than twice the number of students in September of 2011, and it is more than six times the number of students who started at the Auburn School when the campus opened in 2010, with five students, two administrators, a language arts teacher, a social studies teacher, and myself, a math and science teacher. Today I serve as the Auburn School's Social Learning Specialist, a new position the Auburn Team has created, because all of our incredibly bright students have social and communication challenges. Before the Auburn School opened, these students struggled at their previous schools, not because they lacked the intelligence to learn, but because they were misunderstood by their peers and their teachers. With the amazing teamwork of the staff, students, and families, I have helped to grow the amazing model of the Auburn School, which I've seen transform the education and lives of my students, and the students at the other two Auburn campuses. It is my goal to employ scientific research to continue to create, improve, and grow a social and educational model for students with Asperger's and related disorders across the United States.

DEVELOPING THE THEME

The author does an excellent job of introducing a theme that is woven throughout the essay very efficiently. The way in which the author utilizes the theme to draw connections between teaching, research, and advanced degree aspirations is both effective and impressive.

Two is the number of jobs I work this year, and three is the number of days a week I spend at each job. While the nearly 60 hours a week can at times feel overwhelming, I can honestly say that I enjoy every minute as I am fortunate enough to be able to combine my two passions of education and research. After graduating with a BA in Psychology from Georgetown University, I knew that I wanted to become a teacher in order to understand children with autism on a personal level before I entered the research world. Now, I spend every day that I am away from my students as a research associate at the Center for Autism Spectrum Disorders (CASD) in the Pediatric Neuropsychology division of Children's National Medical Center. At CASD, I am a project manager for several studies on cognitive flexibility, executive functioning, and social skills in school-aged children on the autism spectrum. Although my weekends may seem shorter, my weeks do not seem longer because this year I have obtained equilibrium and balance between scientific research and educational practice. My teaching team benefits from the research-based knowledge I bring from CASD, and my research team benefits from the practical advice and applications I bring from Auburn. With this balance, I have solidified my determination to integrate the fields of education and neuropsychology.

One graduate program provides the synergy of science and pedagogy, which I have had to create for myself this year. At the Mind, Brain, and Education Program at Harvard Graduate School of Education, I would collaborate with experts in the fields of biology, cognitive science, and education to refine and answer my questions on creating a model for Asperger's education. The overarching question driving my pursuit of an education in the MBE program is: How does understanding an individual's neurological difference help me create and adapt a learning environment to provide the greatest opportunities for growth and success?

Careful selection of the right classes and professors will help me address and develop several subsets of my overarching question. How do we alleviate the extreme sensory, social, and executive functioning challenges of individuals on the autism spectrum so that they can focus on forming the relationships they desire and achieving the academic potential of which they are capable? MBE core classes, such as Introduction to Education Neuroscience, will provide me with a foundational understanding of the interplay between neuroscience and pedagogy necessary to recognize the root of such challenges. How can one model fit the huge variability among students with social and communication challenges? Classes focusing on individual differentiation and Universal Design for Learning with authorities such as David Rose and Todd Rose will help me tackle that question. Flexibility to take some courses outside of the MBE will allow me to maximize my one year at HGSE by enrolling in classes to address additional interests including Critical Issues in Special Education Policy and Practice. In short, the MBE program provides academic opportunities to address my questions and deepen my understanding of the interconnectedness of science and instruction.

ANSWERING "WHY HARVARD?"

By providing a well-thought-out plan of classes and insight into communication with professors within the program, the author crafts a perfect answer to this question.

Sixteen academic credits a week allows time to engage in extracurricular work and learning activities to focus further on my questions and goals. At the Full Day Open House at HGSE, Dr. Hunter Gehlbach spoke about enhancing social environments and teaching perspective-taking to learners and educators. I immediately knew I wanted to become involved in his research. "How do educators take the perspectives of individuals with special needs?" and "How do we teach individuals with ASD to take perspectives?" are fundamental questions to improving the social and academic experience of learners on the autism spectrum. In several e-mail exchanges with Dr. Gehlbach, we discussed that although his research focuses primarily on neurotypical individuals, it could reasonably be applied to help those with perspective-taking deficits. Just as the MBE program is designed to combine research and practice in its courses, I plan to combine academic studies and practical research in my daily schedule. It is only through approaching my questions with this balance, offered by HGSE, that I will feel confident in working toward my goal to develop a nationwide model for Asperger's education.

Innumerable are the questions I could ask about how best to teach children with Asperger's and related disorders. While each answer to a research question will lead to further questions, each answer will also lead to better strategies to be employed in classrooms around the country. A master's degree from the Mind, Brain, and Education Program at HGSE will equip me to ask the best questions, uncover the best answers, and employ the best strategies for students on the autism spectrum and with other learning needs. While I may brighten a student's day by listing all of the

WRITER'S WORDS OF WISDOM

When I found the MBE program at HGSE I knew it was the perfect program for me and that I was a perfect candidate for it. The trick was making sure the admissions team saw that. As much as I *knew* it, I had to do my research. Adding details about classes I wanted to take, professors with whom I wanted to study, and companies at which I wanted to intern was key to my writing my admissions essay. The research I did not only added to the content of my essay, but it also validated to me the reasons for which I was applying.

prime numbers to 500, I can brighten his future by teaching him the social, sensory, executive functioning, and academic strategies he needs to integrate himself successfully into high school, college, and an independent life.

CHAPTER
38

University of Minnesota
Department of Anthropology

I am interested in the production of public history in New Zealand and the ways it is constituted by and affects matauranga Maori, or Maori forms of knowledge. The Waitangi Tribunal, an official body convened for the purposes of redressing Maori grievances against the state, is the most visible participant in the production of these histories and investigates the colonial archive to construct official narratives of the history of Maori marginalization at the hands of the state. The historical narratives produced by the tribunal have been referred to as "revisionist history" by New Zealand historians and scholars writing on issues of Maori sovereignty and self-determination because of their penchant for judging the actions of historical actors according to modern sensibilities for the purposes of reconciling New Zealand's colonial past with its contemporary image as a bicultural liberal nation state. I am interested in studying the histories produced by the Tribunal, as well as other forms of public history in New Zealand, to uncover the ways in which they have both transformed Maori historical consciousness and informed the development of a contemporary Maori identity. Furthermore, I want to investigate the

WRITING STATEMENTS OF PURPOSE FOR PH.D. PROGRAMS

As you will see within this sample statement for a Ph.D. program, the structure of the Ph.D. statement of purpose differs from the more open-ended formats of other admissions essays in that it should focus on your interest within a certain field of study. The statement provides an opportunity to specify your intended area of concentration, convey your dedication to the subject matter, as well as demonstrate why you are interested in working within the particular department at the university.

influence of these histories on the machinery of advocacy the New Zealand state has developed for mediating Maori-state relations and the ways in which Maori assert their agency as political actors in these encounters as a result of their transformed historical consciousness.

Much of the literature devoted to the issues of Maori self-determination and state sponsored biculturalism has dealt with the political ramifications of these concepts, inquiring into their effects on the New Zealand constitutional order and Maori social policy. Rather than looking at the outcomes of Maori-state encounters and assessing their impact on the advancement of Maori self-determination, I propose to dig deeper and look at the historical origins of Maori-state relations and the epistemological orientations that structure these interactions. Anthropologists such as Thomas Abercrombie, Joanne Rappaport, Marshall Sahlins, and Carolyn Hamilton have written on the issue of indigenous historical consciousness and the ways that cross-cultural interactions transform the structures of historical memory. My project will engage New Zealand in this literature to add another dimension to the debate on biculturalism and Maori self-determination by looking at the ways that the production of public history both enables and constrains the advancement of these concepts within the New Zealand political sphere.

The project I completed at the University of Chicago provided me with a starting point for thinking about many of the issues this work will touch on. I focused on a specific report produced by the Waitangi Tribunal regarding a claim brought by a group of Maori known as Moriori. I found that the Tribunal's process of historicizing the Moriori claim forced Moriori to inhabit an image of themselves rooted in Western social scientific categories for the purposes of achieving legal recognition. Thus, in order to capitalize on their status as indigenous and receive all of the rights and privileges that come with it, Moriori forms of historical consciousness and processes for identity formation were subjugated to Western practices of historicism and legal deter- mination. Given the opportunity to expand upon and develop this project, I would hope to provide an account of Maori practices associated with historical memory and the way those prac- tices have been transformed by participation in Tribunal proceedings. Ultimately, I am inter- ested in how Maori historical knowledge has been transformed by the production of public history in New Zealand.

My interest in the South Pacific began during my undergraduate career, where I took advantage of the courses offered by the Center for Australian and New Zealand Studies at Georgetown University on topics such as New Zealand race relations and the politics of indig- enous visual and performing arts. My interest in the intersections of anthropology and his- tory also took shape during this time, and was enabled by the topic I chose for my BA thesis, which explored the cul- tural implications of colonial rule in Western Samoa. In researching this project, I made extensive use of the Pacific Manuscripts Bureau, which is a collection of documents relating to the history of the Pacific region. In the spring of 2007, I took a semester abroad at Auckland University where I was first exposed to the issues surrounding the Treaty of Waitangi that I later explored in my MA thesis by taking courses on New Zealand history and Maori culture. My graduate education at the University of Chicago allowed me to continue working on the interests I fostered at Georgetown while rounding out my training as an anthropologist

WRITER'S WORDS OF WISDOM

Don't choose a program based solely on its prestige factor. At the graduate level, it is much more important to find a program that fits your interests and needs as a student. Spend some time researching the faculty at different programs to find people whose work will most closely align with yours and contact those people to get a sense of whether or not the department will be a good fit for you.

FORMATTING CONTENT

The author of this essay takes great care to create a successful structure for his statement. Beginning with his proposed plan of research, the author is able to explain his background and subject matter expertise within the particular field, to include where his passion for the material formed and how he has cultivated it to date. Furthermore, the author provides outstanding reasons for his application to the University of Minnesota, citing specific professors and projects that would provide an environment in which the author would be able to thrive.

through courses on anthropological and postcolonial theory and ethnographic fieldwork.

The opportunity to work with the anthropology department at the University of Minnesota will provide the resources I need to carry out this project. David Lipset's work on the intersections of indigenous tradition and modernity in Papua New Guinea would benefit my project by providing me with the theoretical tools to investigate the development of Maori modernity, while the work of Jean Langford on the practice of historical memory in South and Southeast Asia aligns with my interest in the production of public history in New Zealand and its implications for the production of Maori culture. I would be delighted to work with either of these faculty members and feel that the department at the University of Minnesota provides the best fit for my regional and theoretical interests. I firmly believe that the resources and guidance I would receive there would allow me to successfully carry out my proposed project.

CHAPTER
39

Cornell University
School of Hotel Administration

Sally Edwards—triathlon pioneer—has said, "If we're not willing to settle for junk living, we certainly shouldn't settle for junk food." When I graduated from college and moved to New York City, I was settling for both.

I worked for a prestigious public relations firm and lived with two of my best friends in a tiny, mouse and bug-ridden apartment in the East Village. The long work hours meant I often was left eating out of greasy take-out cartons late

at night. I certainly realized I was eating a lot of junk food, but I didn't really care. I was living what I always thought was my dream, but I wasn't happy. Although I didn't realize it at the time, I was "junk living," as Edwards says. My life lacked passion and drive. There was not much, other than the need to pay rent, that got me up in the morning.

I knew my life was missing something, but I wasn't sure what it was. On a quest to lose the pounds I'd gained from all that take-out, I started running along the East River. A mile a day turned into two, then three, and then, on a dare, I signed up to run the Chicago Marathon. On my runs, I began to notice that what I ate during the day affected how fast and how long I could run. I was at my best after eating leafy greens, juicy fruits, rich nuts, and lean meats. After indulging in too much salt, sugar, or oil, I felt horrible. And so the questions began stirring in the grocery store. What are rutabagas? Do I get enough calcium? How do you peel a pineapple? Pomegranates have seeds? The more I learned, the more I wanted to know. My Google history contained questions like "Which beans have the most protein?" and "How do you massage kale?" My mom always cooked at home, and I assumed it was a basic skill that I too possessed. I could stir-fry, but when it came time to soufflé and score, I was lost. I started to research the best ways to cook and bake newly discovered ingredients. What do whipped egg whites look like? What is a frittata?

WRITER'S WORDS OF WISDOM

Be honest.

How do I make gnocchi? I began cooking every night and packing every lunch. Elaborate dishes featuring a cornucopia of roasted veggies and an aquarium of grilled seafood on beds of quinoa risotto or faro started appearing in my lunchbox and dinner table. I felt better than I'd ever felt. I found that what I ate and drank affected my ability to power through 20-mile runs and eventually the Chicago Marathon for 2 years in a row.

I'm still a frequent runner, but I am a fanatic baker and chef. Cooking is my life, and nutrition is my passion. I'd like to combine these interests by working for a restaurant that focuses on fresh, healthy ingredients and inventive flavors. Too often restaurants fail their customers by giving them subpar ingredients that are masked by salt or fat. I believe that bold, rich flavors in small portion sizes are the future of upscale, American dining, and I'm passionate about being a part of this movement. My interest coincides with a rise in the popularity of farm-to-table eating and sourcing local ingredients. I am influenced by pioneers in the industry such as Nora in Washington, DC, and the big names like Blue Hill in New York, but most of all, I'm inspired by the small bistros and restaurants that I grew up dining at in rural Pennsylvania. It is my goal to manage and one day own a restaurant in this vein, and I believe that Cornell's unique Master of Management in Hospitality program will help me develop these skills through its intensive curriculum and strong professional network. The school's wide array of classes that focus on restaurant management, sustainability, and entrepreneurship will help me learn more and hone my vision. I especially am drawn to the ability to tailor your own concentration to meet unique career goals. Cornell's focus on learning from industry leaders through programs like the Dean's Distinguished Lecture Series and the required externship will help me learn more about the field and give me opportunities to develop relationships in the industry. In particular, I was inspired by a recent lecture from Susan Santiago, which focused on Hyatt's health and sustainability initiatives. I also believe that the program's reputation and the incredible alumni network will help me make connections when looking for a position. Finally, I believe that Cornell's unique location in rural New York will be a constant source of inspiration for me. I cannot think of a better place to begin a career that focuses on farm-to-table dining than in the Finger Lakes region. From Moosewood Restaurant to the Farmers' Market, Ithaca is teeming with examples of healthy, fresh cuisine. The numerous vineyards and farms that populate the countryside are amazing examples of enterprises that are supported by locally sourced ingredients.

DETERMINING TONE

The author writes using a casual tone, which is refreshing, but be careful with overusing slang and contractions.

The line of logic presented by Edwards in the quote I referenced argues that living a fulfilling, purposeful life will inspire us to cut out the other junk in our life, most notably junk food, but my journey has been the exact opposite. By cutting out junk food, I found my passion in life. I realized that I could no longer settle for the life I was living in New York. By taking care of my body, I gained the courage to begin to think introspectively about who I am and what I want, and this led me to Cornell.

CHAPTER
40

Columbia University
Teachers College

My Road to the Classroom

On the last day of eighth grade, a gangly and self-conscious girl clings desperately to her English teacher sobbing. That's me. Fresh off the heels of our adventures in *To Kill a Mockingbird* and *The Little Prince*, I could not bear to leave the teacher whose passion for literature inspired my love of reading, discussing, and learning. His class was a safe place for ideas and questions to glide freely through the room. My sense of belonging in the English classroom only deepened when rigorous high school teachers sliced at my verbosity and expanded my vocabulary, and again in college when passionate professors listened to me warmly and guided ideological debates effortlessly. I managed to leave Mr. Goad's side on that last day of middle school, but my fond memories of his teaching and the line of English teachers that succeeded him never faded. I now set my sights on an Initial Certification in the Teaching of English because I hope to inspire in students a lifelong love of reading, writing, and critical thinking as my beloved teachers did for me.

I explored this interest in education during college with volunteer work that revolved almost exclusively around tutoring low-income students in Washington, DC. With the DC Schools project, I was challenged to prepare engaging and creative Language Arts lessons for a struggling ESL eighth grader, where I used music, games, and humorous PowerPoint presentations as writing prompts. As an Operations Intern for Horton's Kids, an educational nonprofit serving students from Anacostia, I provided individual homework help to students grades K–12. Working with such a wide range of ages, I discovered my preference for working with older students and particularly on writing projects. In all of my experience working with children, I felt excited and challenged by the

EXPLAINING A CAREER SHIFT

The personal statement is the perfect place to explain any career changes or shifts in employment that may be apparent on your resume. Here, the author does an excellent job of describing how she pursued one career path, which helped her to discern she may be better suited for a different profession. Her description shows maturity and self-awareness.

task of communicating ideas and helping them succeed in their work. I gained direct classroom experience as the lead teacher for a second grade Sunday school class and again when I took an Elementary Education course at Georgetown, which allowed me to work as a fourth-grade teacher's assistant at an urban public school one day per week. These challenging but valuable experiences taught me a great deal about classroom management and discipline. They also left me longing for the higher level thinking, writing, and critical discussion in high school and college classes.

After college, I took a detour on my path toward teaching to explore my passion for cooking. Weighing the option to attend culinary school, I worked at a chef-driven restaurant and bakery during its first year of operations and ultimately decided that my personality is not a good match with the highly stressful, pressurized life of a chef.

After researching several nearby education programs, Columbia's Teachers College stands alone in programs to prepare superior English teachers. Firstly, the specificity of the coursework—from Teaching of Poetry to Teaching of Shakespeare—offers an opportunity to acquire unequaled expertise managing the unique arena of the English classroom. TC is also unique in offering courses in both pedagogy and literary content. I hope to be a teacher with a sophisticated understanding of literature because I believe it is crucial to help students get the most out of each book they read and inspire higher level thinking. I am excited to take a course or two, if possible, in the renowned English department at Columbia. The structure and support of the fieldwork program is also exciting. For a person like me with vast tutoring experience but less practice in high school classrooms, the easing from assistant teaching during Phase One into lead-teaching two full periods during Phase Two is highly appealing.

CONVINCING THE READER

Through reading this essay, it is clear that Teachers College is the applicant's first choice school. The location and the structure of the program appeal to the author. If this is the case for you, it may be worthwhile to indicate the reasons why the university/program is a strong match for you.

Furthermore, I plan to live and work in the New York metro region, and I believe TC is by far the best school in the region to prepare educators with NY state credentials.

Looking back on my tutoring and volunteer experience, I realize that I possess many of the natural qualities needed to be a great English teacher. I have patience and compassion for everyone I work with, particularly in times when they struggle. I am an engaged and empathetic listener, and I enjoy listening to many different interpretations, opinions, and thoughts. I am naturally encouraging of students' work. Mostly, I love great writing and the lively discussions it can inspire. I believe Columbia's Teachers College is the best place to hone these natural skills and become the type of English teacher I respected and admired throughout my educational journey.

WRITER'S WORDS OF WISDOM

Write from a sincere place, and you'll be fine.

CHAPTER

41

Georgetown University
School of Continuing Studies (Journalism)

"Every Georgetown student wants to change the world." That's the response I got when, as a 17-year-old prospective Georgetown undergraduate, I asked my admissions ambassador to characterize the typical Hoya. At that moment, I knew I was in the right place.

From a very young age, I felt called to speak out against injustice. I was one of two girls on my fourth grade coed soccer team, called "The Molar Men" in homage to the local dental practice that sponsored our uniforms. Not one to silently bear the burden of exclusionary language, I took a tube of White-Out to my jersey, modifying the last word of our team's name with a strategically placed "Wo-." The parents on the sidelines—including my own—were shocked, and all 60-or-so pounds of me beamed with the pride of having stood up for equality, albeit in the smallest of ways.

That fourth grader grew into a zealous undergraduate who moved to DC with wide eyes and a determined spirit, ready to storm the Capitol and figure out how to make our country work for those who'd been left in the dust of our breakneck rise to global influence. While my 5 years in this city have slightly dulled the shine of my idealism, I haven't lost my commitment to social justice or my belief in the transformative power of small, purposeful actions. I know I want to live my life as a "Wo-man for others." The question, in a world as complex and confusing as ours, is: How?

EXPRESSING INDIVIDUALITY

The author engages the reader from the onset by choosing a memorable anecdote that makes her essay stand out.

One of my Georgetown professors, a close mentor and friend, once shared with me a powerful quote from philosopher and civil rights activist Howard Thurman:

"Don't ask yourself what the world needs," said Thurman. "Ask yourself what makes you come alive and then go do that. Because what the world needs is people who have come alive."

For me, writing isn't just a passion. It's an imperative. Writing breeds in me both a sense of personal freedom and a warm feeling of connection to my community. When I buckle down to shape disjointed facts into a meaningful narrative, I use both sides of my brain in a way that energizes me to the core. I come alive.

My love of writing and my insatiable curiosity led me to the field of journalism. The essence of journalism is storytelling, a mode of communication as ancient as speech itself. A well-told story not only engages the reader or listener; it enrages, excites, and challenges her. It answers some questions, but inspires far more. I found my niche in storytelling while filming a documentary on a DC needle exchange organization for my American Studies thesis project. During my 5 months of research, interviews, filming, and editing, I met dozens of women and men whose stories exhibited incredible strength, perseverance, selflessness, and faith—and often revealed the incompetence of our current HIV prevention systems. Yet, without my amateur filmmaking attempt, these stories would have never reached the eyes or ears of anyone outside of this insular community of HIV-positive individuals dealing with homelessness, drug use, and imprisonment, much less the policymakers and healthcare workers who needed to hear their stories most.

Though my thesis work certainly didn't strengthen our city's commitment to needle exchange funding, it gave me renewed confidence in my desire and ability to tell untold stories and seek out voices that have been historically suppressed. Visual media and the written word are powerful tools in the dissemination of truth, and I want to use journalism to bring hidden truths to light. This master's program will allow me to develop the skills in research, interviewing, and writing that I'll need to be an effective and ethical reporter in the pursuit of our society's most uncomfortable truths. It will also benefit my work as Alumni Communications Manager at Georgetown's Office of Advancement. Telling stories about our students, alumni, and campus community is at the core of my job. The training I'll get in news and feature writing will have an immediate impact on the work I produce on behalf of the university.

Experimenting with new media platforms in my work at Advancement has taught me that standard print practices don't always work in the digital realm—a lesson learned through painstaking analytics research and a review of alumni usage patterns. Over the past year, I've spearheaded efforts to revamp our alumni website with multimedia and interactive content that uses social media to engage a broad spectrum of alumni. As an aspiring journalist, I'm eager to learn about the intersection of print and digital media in today's news consumption climate. I want to improve my judgment in identifying newsworthy stories and finding the most effective ways to share them, be it through traditional channels or new media.

With a background in nonfiction filmmaking, newspaper journalism, and communications, I have a skill set that will be broadened and deepened by the challenges that this master's program provides. Balancing a full-time job with coursework will take discipline and focus,

> **WRITER'S WORDS OF WISDOM**
>
> I worked full time at Georgetown while getting my degree at night, so all of my classes were free. If you don't want to take out loans for grad school, I would recommend looking for jobs at the university you'd like to attend—it might offer tuition as a benefit.

two traits I honed in college when I took on an independent film project during the final semester of my senior year. My inquisitive mind, sharp eye for a compelling story, and commitment to the pursuit of truth in service of justice will support my developing skills as a journalist. A healthy dose of audacity, as evidenced by my fourth-grade soccer jersey alteration, keeps me unafraid to broach the difficult topics that a journalist needs to explore in today's uncertain, ever-shrinking world.

I'm convinced that my admissions ambassador was right, that every Georgetown student wants to change the world. Each of us does it in our own unique way, and storytelling is mine. With a master's in journalism, I'll have the foundation of expertise I'll need to effect positive change by amplifying the unheard voices of our society.

CHAPTER

42

University of Southern California

Dornslife College of Letters, Arts and Sciences (Statistics)

I have always had an affinity for math, numbers, and finding answers. I discovered I was a "left-brained" student sometime during middle school and took much pleasure in my calculus courses throughout high school. But never did I consider pursuing a career in mathematics until my quantitative studies at Georgetown University took my knowledge to a previously unknown level. I was able to apply my raw interest to higher order socioeconomic principles. It was through econometrics and applied statistics courses that I discovered my fascination for interpreting economic and social phenomena with statistical data and models. Statistics is the critical mathematical science used to summarize and explain data, and I relish the stories that statistics tell through measurable pieces of information. As a result of these stories, it provides an essential tool in any research realm, be it financial, psychological, sociological, economical, etc. In May 2010, I graduated from Georgetown University with degrees in economics and mathematics. Through this experience and

COMMUNICATING A LOVE OF LEARNING

While brainstorming potential essay topics, you may want to consider which undergraduate courses you enjoyed the most and more importantly, what it was about them that piqued your interest. Here, the author clearly pinpoints the beginning of her passion for statistics and thoughtfully declares how she hopes to channel this passion through pursuing graduate studies.

my continuing interest in practical economics, I have come to realize the incredible utility a master's degree in statistics from USC will provide beyond my present experience.

Specifically, my deeper goal in pursuing this graduate work is to gain an understanding of modern statistical theory and practices in order to pursue a career in an area of research I find particularly fascinating, behavioral economics. Behavioral economics is the observational study of how individuals act in the marketplace, regardless of what classical economic theory may dictate. As a statistician with a vested interest in this research, I would be an asset to companies, governments, schools, and households that require this type of analysis to make more informed and strategic fiscal decisions. My passion for research in business decision-making and behavioral economics primarily stems from self-study of books written by Dan Ariely, a pioneer in analyzing the role human irrationality plays within economics. While reading Ariely's experimental work that examines many forms of human decision-making, I found myself particularly intrigued by his insight into how people reason with regards to financial choices. For example, in his 2003 study entitled, "Coherent Arbitrariness: Stable Demand Curves Without Stable Preferences," Ariely presents convincing statistical evidence to indicate that traditional market demand curves do not often reflect true consumer preferences and pricing valuations, which are often determined by arbitrary variables. In this way and many more, traditional economic theory is limited in how it can inform real-time financial and marketing decisions. It has become apparent to me that observation of real human behavior is necessary to build off of this foundation. Rigorous analysis of human behavior requires the use of statistics. My role and contributions as a statistician, research analyst, and consultant will be valuable to many, including economists, politicians, entrepreneurs, and business owners.

Thus far, my academic experience in economics has been primarily theory-based. However, I have seen that this way of thinking can be very limiting in the actual marketplace through my extensive work experience as an assistant manager (and accounting guru) at lululemon athletica, an expanding, yoga-inspired athletic apparel company. The research conducted to understand the consumer behavior of its well-defined market niche and the statistical analysis employed to then create its effective business model are key to the company's burgeoning success. My management position at the company allowed me to implement the findings of this process and directly experience the value it had. This work experience, along with my educational curriculum, helped to clearly define my next educational endeavor, a master's degree in statistics.

I am drawn specifically to USC's program because not only will it provide me with a strong statistics foundation, but it will also present unique interdisciplinary research opportunities that will prepare me for a career in applied statistics and quantitative research. In addition, I would be honored to study with Dr. John Doe focusing on financial mathematics, as well as Dr. Jane Smith from the economics department with research interests in behavioral economics. During my undergraduate career, I took a solid course load that has undoubtedly prepared me for graduate study in statistics and applied mathematics. I believe my natural quantitative abilities and ever-growing passion to apply knowledge of statistics and economics to specific research initiatives qualify me as an ideal candidate for the Master's Program in Statistics at USC.

WRITER'S WORDS OF WISDOM

Talk to people. Before you begin the application process to graduate school, reach out to those who fully understand what you may be getting yourself into—this may include current students, graduates now in the workforce, as well as professors within those programs of interest. Graduate school is a world beyond that of your undergraduate experience, and it requires your full attention and commitment. Ask yourself the following questions: Is this degree crucial to my being successful in my career? Am I truly interested in the subject matter or am I buying time to figure out what it is that I really want to do? Be 100% certain that graduate school is the next step for you.

CHAPTER

43

Columbia University
Teachers College, Summer Principals Academy

We stood—a small, motley group of parents, children, and teachers—rolling bright, warm stripes of paint onto the dismal gray walls of our school's entryway. Though our conversation came in halts and bursts of English and Spanish, our purpose united us, as we worked to transform a space from hopeless to inspiring. The entryway to the school is an important place. For years, it had been the door from a neighborhood which had long disowned it, associating the school with violence, academic failure, and a sense of low expectations.

Since our school's founding in 2009, it is where our teachers pass each morning, breathlessly chattering about the plans for the day; where excited children eagerly hurry into the warm, embracing fold of their school family; where parents are met and greeted as they arrive for meetings; where families cross as they arrive to proudly watch our students excitedly take the stage to perform.

CRAFTING A STRONG HOOK

The author invites you into his story by taking you right through the entrance of his school. This is a strong introduction that surely stands out in a pile of personal statements.

The project was a small one in comparison to many of the roles I have taken on in my time at PS 317 Waterside Children's Studio School, but it captures some essential qualities of my leadership. First, I saw a problem—in this case, the blank, gray walls of a school long associated with failure and low expectations—and envisioned the solution and the potential for transformation. Bringing vision to reality, I applied for and was awarded grant funding; created the designs; gathered volunteers; purchased supplies; and managed schedules and permits. I rolled up my sleeves and painted side by side with a team of stakeholders in our school's success—parents, staff, and students. We were left with blocks of bright, vivid colors, and the words "PS 317: Learn. Create. Imagine" covering the walls. "It makes me feel hopeful," one mother told us. It had become an entryway which could signify to everyone who walks through our doors that they will be empowered with the tools they need to succeed to their very greatest potential.

My first year as a teacher was also PS 317's first year as a new DOE school replacing a failed phase-out in a uniquely challenging community. When I applied to Teach for America 4 years ago, I was a Georgetown University Social Justice Analysis student working in DC's homeless community. I wrote in my application essay about how my experiences had taught me that "no one should ever give up his or her struggle against injustices large or small, no matter how hopeless or frustrating a situation may seem. For every person that fights to make the world a better and more just place does so simply by fighting." In my time teaching since then as part of the inaugural team of teachers at Far Rockaway's PS 317 Waterside Children's Studio School, I have had the opportunity to meet, work with, and learn from many such fighters. I saw firsthand the tremendous impact passionate leaders, including our founding principal, can have in that fight to make the world better—in the classroom, throughout the school, and in the greater Far Rockaway community. The realization that my own impact could be multiplied as a school leader quickly became apparent.

As I learned to create and implement positive behavior plans and design rigorous, individualized instruction for students in my self-con-

tained third-grade classroom, I was also participating in key schoolwide decisions as we shaped
our mission, modified and adapted our curriculum, and built engagement with our children's
families and the larger community. As our
school grew and developed in mission, capacity, and impact, so did I. Beyond the leadership
role I stand in daily as a special education classroom teacher to the part I've played in logisti-
cal, operational, and instructional planning for
the school, I have had the opportunity to learn
and grow through many different leadership
opportunities.

WRITER'S WORDS OF WISDOM

My advice to applicants would be to heed Rumi's advice of "Let the beauty of what you love be what you do." If you are letting the beauty you love be what you do, that sense of passion and purpose should frame your essay.

The school we had replaced had long failed its students; the most
affected by this failure were the students with special needs. As a proactive approach, I partnered with another classroom teacher to focus and
strengthen our support for struggling learners as Coordinators of Special
Education. This has been perhaps the most important, formative role I
have had the opportunity to take on. Through my work, I have learned
that leaders must be strong at proactively building structures and systems
to create a successful environment in which children can learn and must
also be able to respond thoughtfully and comprehensively to situations
as they arise. Through participating in and eventually leading focused,
practical, and impactful professional development, as well as small group
and individual coaching and support, I have learned about, shared, and
helped to implement positive behavioral and academic interventions and
strategies which have made our school a place where all students can
learn, grow, and feel valued. I created a video library of teachers within
our school, filming, editing, and compiling clips of my colleagues at
work to maximize the impact of sharing best practices for supporting all
of our learners. The results are not only in our testing scores, which show
dramatic progress among our lowest third, but in the smiling faces of
our students, in the pages of their writing which adorn our walls, in the
excited whispers of their reading in classroom libraries.

Our special education students and the lowest third of our learners are not the only underserved among our student population. For years, local schools have failed our community. It is an extraordinarily urgent level of investment required to fight for these students—I remembered that each role that I took on at the school had the potential to be a key piece of the fight for those not yet old enough to fight for themselves. Whether it was fundraising (more than $250,000 for a new technology lab, auditorium renovation, playground, and beautification projects like our entryway); collaborating with our school's Parent Teacher Association; forming partnerships with community leaders and our local City Councilman; writing and planning new curriculum maps across content areas aligned with the new Common Core Standards; or supporting instructional and behavioral best practices in classrooms throughout the school—I constantly had in mind the value each result would have on the learning, well-being, and success of our children.

Summer Principals Academy, I believe, is the next step in my training to be a fighter for educational equity for all children. For 3 years, I have had the powerful experience of helping to lead a brand new school under what many in our community told us were impossible circumstances. We worked relentlessly each day to raise student achievement, to foster stakeholder investment, and to reflect on and improve our own instruction and pedagogy. Summer Principals Academy would allow me to continue this important work at PS 317 while developing my potential and maximizing my future effectiveness. I believe and have seen that school leaders have the ability to make a tremendous promise to children that school can and will change their life and build their future. In this promise—which I believe Summer Principals Academy can help me make—I know there is also a battle won in the fight toward making the world a better and more just place.

PROVIDING THE SOLUTION

After presenting a symbolic and well-written introduction and describing the conflict, the author now faces the task of explaining how his graduate studies focus fits into the long-term resolution, which he successfully provides here.

CHAPTER

44

University of Pennsylvania
Department of Romance Languages

Amiri Baraka's iconic Black Arts Movement poem, "Black Art," published in 1966 opens with the statement, "Poems are bullshit unless they are/ teeth or trees or lemons piled/ on a step." My second year as an undergraduate, this poem caused a completely unexpected and seismic shift in my perception of literature's role in society. In class one afternoon, I volunteered to read "Black Art" aloud, without having read it before. The jarringly violent and vulgar images the words created as I read them, accompanied by the incredulity that I was the one speaking them into existence, produced obvious visceral reactions in the whole class. For me, that instant made undeniable the fact that, while a poem clearly conveys ideas, it also quite evidently constitutes an action. In a sense, it shocked me into the realization that poetic texts, like all literary texts, do not simply say things; the action Baraka's poem not only calls for but also takes itself manifests the roles texts play as dynamic interventions in the world they come into.

My interest in studying literature owes a great part of its genesis to that moment; its emphasis on reading theory with literature and, at times, literature as theory, confirms what I find so vital about art: its capacity, on which Baraka's poem clearly insists, to be and do something real, and to intervene in its context. These ideas have also motivated my choice of focus within literary studies, inspired in part by a fascination with the complex relationship between Latin America and the United States, and the political and economic history of mutual influence that these regions share. Hence, I study twentieth century and contemporary Latin American, Brazilian, and United States literatures in Spanish, Portuguese, and English, with an emphasis on trans-American readings and on analysis of the tensions and possibilities specific to sites of contact between these regions.

As a Master's student in Comparative Literature, I have worked to ensure I have a comprehensive foundation for moving forward with my thesis project and plans for doctoral studies. I have gained familiarity with contemporary Latin American literature through seminars with Leila Gómez and Peter Elmore, and am continuing to study lusophone and Brazilian literature in Portuguese language and Brazilian literature courses. The Survey of Literary Theory and Enlightenment Aesthetics courses with Eric White and Christopher Braider, as well as Henry Pickford's Foundations of Critical Theory and the Critical Theory of the Frankfurt School seminars will, I hope, confirm my competence with regard to the groundwork of critical and literary theories today. Because I focus on work from the twentieth and twenty-first centuries, I think an established understanding of its intellectual antecedents is crucial. The time I have spent working on this MA has proven indispensable not only for my under-

CREATING FLOW

The structure of the statement can vary based on the topic you choose and your preferred way of presenting it. Note the natural flow of this essay as it carries the theme through chronologically from bachelor's degree to master's degree to intended doctoral studies. Organizing material through a timeline is an example of one structural approach; however, the most important aspect to consider is how well the essay flows, which this essay certainly does.

standing of the origins of contemporary work, but also in illuminating the new possibilities it can open up.

In my ongoing MA thesis project I use post- and de-colonial theories and conceptions of queer temporality to analyze Junot Díaz's novel, *The Brief Wondrous Life of Oscar Wao*. In doing so, I attempt to illustrate how the alienation that Díaz's characters experience as a result of life in Diaspora, between the Dominican Republic and the United States, not only extends to culture and linguistics, but also sets them in contrast to normative temporal figurations of past, present, and future. I argue that Oscar, through his persistent inability to find sexual partners, ultimate failure to reproduce, and sui- cide attempt troubles and challenges (hetero) normative figurations of successful life trajecto- ries, the emphases of which are longevity and reproductive sexuality. I hope to explain how queer theory can prove useful in understanding experiences of hybridity and alienation even in contexts where queer sexualities as such do not necessarily appear as central, and simultaneously endeavor to read Díaz's characters as relevant to discussions of queer temporality.

As I continue my research, I plan to focus on literature that brings directly into play the particular significance of languages, experiences, and lives that exist in between and outside of normative conceptions and categories, in work from Latin America and the U.S., and from sites of contact between the two, such as writing from the Latin American Diaspora, literature

WRITER'S WORDS OF WISDOM

Whenever anyone has asked me for suggestions for graduate school applications, the first thing I tell them (and, really, what I think is the most important for success) is to make sure they can identify a specific person on the faculty of every program they're applying to that they'd want to work with, to be able to articulate why, and then to get in direct contact with that person to express interest and try to get a dialogue going. For me, it was immensely useful to be able to correspond with people in each program I applied to for many reasons. First of all, while someone's interests as described on the website might look like they line up with yours, you might find out after asking more specific questions that really their approach doesn't fit what you're looking for. Alternately, you could find out that they'd actually be ideal, or even that you have more interests and ideas in common with them than you could have known from the website. It's also a good

continues on page 194

continued from page 193
way to find out what kind of advisor they might be; you might find, after trying to get in touch with them, that they really don't respond well to emails, that they don't find your research interests to be in line with theirs, that they're not taking on more students at that point, etc., and you can direct your focus to other programs. Or, again, you could find that they're very attentive and that they find your research interests extremely fruitful and provocative. Basically, getting in touch with them can only help you by giving you more information about the faculty members, and if you're able to create a relationship with them before applying, you'll then have someone in the program who can be an advocate for you when the time to review applications appears for them. I personally know that these correspondences played a huge role in where I ended up and I know that I ended up making the best possible decision with the most possible information as a result of them.

from the U.S.-Mexico Border and Puerto Rico, and works that emphasize, address, or enact multiculturality. I am interested in using queer theory, along with narratology and postcolonial work, to explore how analyses of linguistic, cultural, and identical ambiguity can illuminate the alternatives and possibilities that these literatures present and create.

The Program in Hispanic Studies at the University of Pennsylvania would be ideal for me for several reasons. The structure of the program, which emphasizes a special area of theoretical interest in addition to literary specializations, would allow me to explore in depth the application of queer theory in studies of narration and themes in literary works. I have had the opportunity to correspond at length with Dr. Román de la Campa this summer and fall about my research interests and doctoral studies plans and was fortunate enough to meet with him in person this November to discuss the possibility of working together. I find his work on Latin American, U.S., and Latino literatures clearly relevant and consequential and feel that I would benefit immensely from studying with him and, of course, the many other scholars on your faculty.

I hope you will consider me for a place in your program and sincerely appreciate your time.

CHAPTER 45

Georgetown University
Communication, Culture & Technology

Only 30 minutes have passed since our bus left the hotel in Seoul, but the view from my window is already losing the capital city's vibrancy. The warm hues emanating from its electric skyline have given way to a steel-gray overcast; the neon spectrum of small stylish cars I've gotten accustomed to vanishes, and now convoys of armored infantry trucks stretch along lanes of the highway on both sides of us. Just beyond the barbed wire fences that line the road to Panmunjom, the vegetation abruptly stops, revealing the barren surface on the other side. There are no trees, our tour guide begins to explain, because the North Koreans have cut and burned them all for fuel.

My daytrip to the demilitarized zone between South and North Korea the summer after college was my own personal capstone to the semesters I had devoted to understanding the needs of postconflict societies. I had diced up the course catalog to assemble my own curriculum, debated in diplomacy simulations around the nation, and pored over international legal briefs with professors during their office hours. In the end, I graduated from Georgetown University's School of Foreign Service with an expert sensibility about transitional environments. Stories from Rwanda, Yugoslavia, and Afghanistan leapt off the pages as I studied the critical points where punishment met reconciliation and international law met local custom. Helping a society that had been torn apart by years of ethnic conflict find sustainable peace requires creative and comprehensive solutions, and I am fascinated and emboldened by the challenge.

Yet what I found in my visit to Korea was not the postconflict case study I had expected, but a vivid canvas of design and technology in action. My perspective as an international relations student was shifting, colored by the extensive portfolio I had built up as the primary graphic designer for more than 40 of Georgetown's student-run events and organizations. Seoul's marketplaces teemed with young artists eager to share their vision for Korea through their work. Elaborate monuments and memorials, rich with multimedia and digital art, beautifully captured Korea's turbulent history and illustrated its steadfast hope that its two halves would become whole again. I photographed, sketched, and blogged every minute of my trip, ever-intrigued by Korea's cutting-edge reinterpretation of its historical narrative. Through the experience, I discovered that this was an area where my own two halves—part artist, part analyst—could come

WRITER'S WORDS OF WISDOM

Getting a master's degree part-time while working a demanding full-time job is no easy feat, but if you're passionate about what you intend to study, the time and energy will be well worth it. I enjoyed applying for CCT because it gave me opportunities to showcase my passion creatively—in addition to the personal statement, they asked for a short video introduction. I ended up going the extra mile by designing and animating a video that told my story, and I'm so glad I put in that additional effort. When I get stressed about the combined pressures of work, school, and life outside of it, I can re-watch that video or re-read my essay to remind myself that choosing this tough path was the right one for creating a career driven by passion.

together, too, and found myself back in DC a week later to explore that intersection. I never left.

It has been over a year since I returned to Georgetown as an alumnus, trading in my textbooks and term papers for a cubicle and project briefs. As the interactive communications manager for the Office of Advancement, I use web applications and social media to help Georgetown build its community beyond its campus. I have worked closely with designers, programmers, fundraisers, administrators, writers, and many others to help push Georgetown's digital identity forward, and, in doing so, have been involved in projects from conception to coding. Though the technical skills I am developing have helped me make an impact at my alma mater, my dedication to learning about technology and its role in building community relates to serving the greater purpose I began to understand while in Korea. I believe that, with the right mentorship, I can make a transformative impact on communities in transition, and that learning from the world-class faculty and students in the Communication, Culture & Technology program at Georgetown will make this possible.

CHAPTER

46

Northwestern University

Medill School of Journalism, Media, Integrated Marketing Communications

Please upload a document that tells us in 500 words or less what factors and influences have moved you toward a career in journalism. How have you pursued this career so far, and what are your goals? All applicants are encouraged to provide links to online examples of their work.

My dad is a stockbroker and my mom is a nurse. The majority of my relatives are either bankers or nurses. Clearly the idea of being a journalist was not instilled in me at birth. Instead, I grew up with an interest in the news and current events, specifically international relations, which came as a result of multiple moves between the U.S. and London during my childhood. During high school, I signed up for a journalism class where

The author breaks down
the daunting task of
starting the essay by using
a brainstorming technique.
By thinking about two
critical elements of "how
have I pursued my goals
so far" and "what are my
future goals," the author
is able to start typing and
make progress on a very
comprehensive essay. See
the author's brainstorming
notes below:
- How have I pursued my
  goals so far?
  » High school
    newspaper
  » Summers—London
    internship
  » Georgetown — the
    Hoya, developed
    working relationships
    with my beat
  » Abroad — Junior Year
    Abroad Network
  » Georgetown again
    — wanted to do
    something different,
    enjoy editing on The
    Hoya and friends'
    papers; worked with
    professor on his book;
    local paper

we produced the school's monthly paper. Since that fateful elective, I have known that I wanted a career in journalism.

Journalism classes in both high school and college are helpful ways to learn the basics, but the best way to improve your writing and research skills is through practice. In that vein, internships at news organizations of different shapes and sizes have helped me to learn about the industry. I have interned at *The Sunday Times* in London over the course of three summers, where I worked on the News, News Review, and Motoring desks. This gave me the chance to see how a part of an international newspaper is run at a very early age.

At Georgetown University, I worked at *The Hoya*, the campus newspaper, starting out as a staff writer on the student government beat and progressing up to the position of City News Editor where I managed and trained a staff of writers. While abroad in Strasbourg, France, I was a part of Georgetown's Junior Year Abroad Network, writing critical essays about the relationship between religion and politics in the city. When I returned to campus, I took my red pen and edited a professor's book manuscript about the relationship between American politics and the media. I spent last summer working at a neighborhood newspaper in Washington, *The Current Newspapers*. Due to the small size of the publication, I was given a great amount of responsibility and wrote three articles per issue. This year I am a research assistant for Mary Jordan, a Pulitzer-Prize winning journalist at *The*

BRAINSTORMING
CONTINUED

Further brainstorming
notes:
- What are my goals?
  » To become a good
    writer, be able to
    tell the untold story,
    to find the untold
    story and paint a
    picture with words. To
    transport the reader.

Washington Post, which is giving me an inside look into the process of producing detailed features pieces. My most recent journalistic endeavor is the creation of a restaurant review blog, serving as a way to combine two of my passions (writing and eating) as well as familiarize myself with ways to gain an audience through new media.

WRITER'S WORDS OF WISDOM

It should come as no surprise that writers are some of the harshest critics when it comes to reading someone else's work. View the essay as an opportunity to highlight your writing skills: show how smoothly you can weave your life's story into just one page. It may only be 500 words, but you want to leave them wanting to know so much more.

Journalism is essentially storytelling. I want to become the best storyteller that I can, finding the most interesting, unusual stories and using my words to paint a picture for the reader.

CHAPTER
47

University of Dayton
Department of
Religious Studies

I hope to pursue a Master of Arts in theological studies at the University of Dayton so as to continue an educational journey that began in college. While an undergraduate at Georgetown, I double-majored in history and Arabic. My collegiate experience taught me the importance of "context" in terms of understanding the development of ideas that guide social, political, and religious movements. In a similar fashion, my young career as a teacher has highlighted the value of "connections" in celebrating both the commonalities and divergent characteristics of world cultures. As a graduate student, I hope to apply and develop both the skills of context and connection to my study of Christianity. Ultimately, I want to answer the questions of "What do Christians around the world believe, and how did they arrive at these beliefs?"

As I progressed through core and major requirements during college, I became increasingly fascinated with Islam and the development of Islamic movements. I enrolled in Middle Eastern and Mediterranean history survey and seminar courses, met with my professors frequently, and eventually, garnered a research assistant position in the Georgetown

Undergraduate Research Opportunities Program (GUROP). I researched modern Islamic political movements under the tutelage of Professor Yvonne Haddad. I found myself drawn to the contextual origins and religious foundations of these movements—in particular, Hizbollah. The following summer (2009), I applied for a GUROP Fellowship to examine Hizbollah's history and guiding theological framework. As I continued my research during my senior year while composing my senior honors thesis in history, I focused on how historical events—the Israeli invasions in 1978 and 1982 and the Islamic Revolution in Iran—

USING STRONG VERBS

Underscore, reaffirm, and *concentrate* are a few of the verbs the author has chosen to convey his message. The author uses sophisticated language without making it sound at all forced.

encouraged the formation of a Shi'ite political and paramilitary organization guided by Iran's Ayatollah Khomeini and bent on expelling the Israeli occupation force. My thesis certainly reaffirmed the critical nature of understanding context with regard to religious movements.

As a social studies and English teacher, I have the privilege of teaching the area's best and brightest. Perhaps the most difficult part of my position consists of challenging these students to think more deeply and broadly. In the early weeks of my World Civilizations course—a year-long requirement for all freshmen—I fervently push my students to make "connections." These connections may appear as cause-and-effect relationships; for instance, how did increased iron-working technology impact the development of faith systems? Or, these connections may seem to be peculiar similarities that transcend boundaries of geography, time, and creed, such as the common railing against social injustices by Jesus, Buddha, and Muhammad. I've come to appreciate this way of learning and seeing the world as an interconnected web rather than group of isolated continents. The way I teach underscores my intellectual curiosity and, in turn, my drive to learn the relationships connecting belief systems.

Both my development as a student and teacher reflect my emerging interest in religious studies. Although I have concentrated my energies on the realm of Islamic studies up to this point, I would like to branch out to

Christian theological studies at the master's level. Through UD"s "Foundation Courses," I will develop a fuller understanding of Christianity's contextual origins and widely held beliefs—in short, I will begin to arrive at answers to my aforementioned questions. With a combined background in Islam and Christianity, I plan on pursuing a Ph.D. in comparative religion with a specific emphasis Muslim-Christian relations. One look at the news has shown us the dire need for scholars who can build bridges of dialogue connecting the Muslim and Christian worlds. I hope to contribute to this conversation by discovering areas of common ground while also celebrating the differences that make these groups distinctive.

WRITER'S WORDS OF WISDOM

Why did I choose to go to graduate school? Simply put, I like school and all of its trappings. I like reading—even if I can't always understand what I'm reading. I like visiting professors during their office hours. I like writing essays that force me to re-process the readings and discussions and come up with something of my own. Unsurprisingly, choosing to go to graduate school was easy for me.

CHAPTER

48

University of St Andrews
School of English

The novels *Wuthering Heights* and *The Tenant of Wildfell Hall* by Emily Bronte and Anne Bronte, respectively struck a chord with many Victorians due to what many saw as the immorality inherent in both novels. While Emily Bronte's novel does not condemn its characters for their moral depravity, Anne Bronte's does; *The Tenant of Wildfell Hall* is a novel quite clear in its belief that alcoholism and debauchery are very immoral and very inappropriate. Yet, the critics still attacked it as being rather wicked; though she moralized, Anne Bronte still brought up issues that society did not wish to discuss. I want to know why presenting debauchery was still considered in poor taste.

There must be more to the critics' claims of immorality and indecency, aside from obvious

WRITER'S WORDS OF WISDOM

Choose what you love. Think about your passions, your curiosities, your interests, and run with them. Are you passionate about 16th century art? Get a master's in it. Do you love innovation and emerging markets? Earn a degree in it. Do you think it would be interesting to delve into metaphysics? Go for it. Your education will always be yours—no one else's! So don't worry about jobs and markets and economies and ROIs. Everything will fall into place—you might as well enjoy the ride!

initial discomfort. Were the novels too close to truth in some areas? If so, which? Is it worse to be a "widow" and condemn debauchery, than to be a Catherine and subsist in it? Is morality dependent on a particular patriarchal structure? Does the criticism surrounding these novels lend support to this notion, or undermine it? What do these novels say about the society they were written in? Can they, being written by women, say anything about society? How did society—the institution of marriage, the patriarchy—influence the topics of and themes within these novels?

I have an unquenchable curiosity to know more about how literature operates, why it is so addictive, and what I can do to further my knowledge of a discipline that so enthralls me. When I was just 8 years old I remember looking up to the top shelf of my mother's bookcase to see the deep green cover of her copy of Emily Bronte's *Wuthering Heights*. Ever since that moment, my attention has been consumed by novels, poems, plays, and any piece of text I can get my hands on. William Blake, Jane Austen, and the Bronte sisters became quick favorites, as did Charles Dickens, George Eliot, and Oscar Wilde.

These authors continue to fascinate me. There is something so fundamentally human about the texts of these authors themselves that continuously pulls me toward another read: I am a fly on the wall in *Middlemarch*, I run with Lizzie through inches of mud, and what I feel when reading *Wuthering Heights* can only be described as sublime. These works of art have shaped me. They have made me aware of the power of words put together in just such a way, of the control emotion holds over a text and a reader, and of the import seemingly innocuous references have on a text and on a modern reader.

At Warwick I will read for the MA in English: Romantic and Victorian Literature, with a focus on the Victorian period. I will study both the culture and society of the Victorian period, as well as the influence of gender and sexuality on morality within literature and society. Accordingly, I will read the Core Modules "Condition of England: Perceptions in Victorian Literature" and "Sexual Geographies: Gender and Place in British Fiction, 1840–1940" in addition to the Foundation Module, "Introduction to Research Methods." For Critical Theory, I will read "Psychoanalysis and Literary Criticism" and "Postmodernism, Marxism, Deconstruction." These modules, combined with my inquisitiveness, will further solidify my knowledge in this field as I examine the intricate manner in which morality weaves through literature and society through the lens of gender and sexuality.

WRITER'S WORDS OF WISDOM

Logistics—be strategic! Choose your passion, find the top five programs in the country and/or the world, research, research, research! Contact the graduate secretary, ask current students for opinions and advice, read the program director's bio and works—this particular part will help to ensure the program is a good fit for you! Analyze the writing style of your chosen programs—they should have current masters/doctoral theses/dissertations on file and accessible, at least in partial form, then put your current fabulous education to work and write a phenomenal statement of purpose tailored to your interests and the program's ethos. You'll get you into the program of your dreams!

DISPLAYING ENTHUSIASM

Keep in mind what admissions officers are looking for in applicants . . . certainly a demonstrated interest in the subject matter and desire to learn are at the top of the list of criteria. The author highlights her limitless curiosity and provides admissions officers with insight into the level of enthusiasm she would bring to the program.

Georgetown University
Security Studies Program

As a Paralegal Specialist in the Office of International Affairs at the U.S. Department of Justice, I am uniquely situated at the cross-roads of the U.S. criminal justice system and the world of foreign policy. I coordinate between state and federal law enforcement, a variety of federal agencies, and foreign governments. This experience offers me perspective on careers in a number of fields, most notably law, law enforcement, foreign policy, national security, and intelligence. In comparing these potential career paths, I have decided to pursue a career in which I make policy decisions in the interest of U.S. national security. I am convinced that a Master of Arts in Security Studies from Georgetown University will best allow me to achieve that goal.

DEMONSTRATING MATURITY

People go to graduate school for a number of reasons; make sure your essay conveys that you are there for the right ones. Here, the author carefully articulates how he has used his prior work experience to identify his interests and to cultivate a skill set geared toward a career in national security. The author also conveys why he believes the program will help him advance his personal career goals.

Prior to working at the Department of Justice, I earned a Bachelor of Science in Foreign Service from Georgetown. My undergraduate studies established a solid academic foundation in the area of international relations, and I put that knowledge into practice in my professional capacity. Through my tenure at the Department of Justice, I have also gained an understanding of the importance of law-enforcement efforts on national

security. The most interesting and rewarding part of my job is analyzing the impact of our case-specific decisions on broader U.S. national security objectives. For instance, our office must determine how an extradition request for a high-level drug trafficker fits into the overarching counter-narcotics strategy of the United States. I enjoy assessing the impact of these decisions and making recommendations based on their national security implications.

A Master of Arts in Security Studies will complement both my undergraduate studies and my practical experience. Ultimately, I intend to transition to a position in which I evaluate intelligence and make policy decisions to protect the United States from threats posed by transnational organized crime. Diplomatic and law-enforcement efforts against violent international drug-trafficking networks are of particular interest to me. A master's degree in security studies will prepare me to transition successfully onto this career path.

The Security Studies Program at Georgetown is ideally positioned to maximize the benefit of my graduate studies. The university's reputation and location attract a variety of exceptionally talented individuals, and learning from professors who continue to practice in their respective fields is invaluable. In addition, the Georgetown community extends into a wide range of government agencies, which will prove beneficial as I seek to continue a career in the public sector. These qualities are the key components of the competitive advantage that a degree from Georgetown's Security Studies Program offers, and they are the principal motivators of my desire to return to Georgetown.

In conclusion, my professional experience has demonstrated to me that a master's degree from the Security Studies Program at Georgetown University is central to my future career ambitions. It is the missing piece on my academic résumé, and I seek admission to the program to complete the foundation for my career.

CHAPTER

50

University of Southern California
School of Cinematic Arts

Growing up, I always had a curious mind and a thirst for information. Much to the frustration of my parents, I was always asking abstract questions, presenting my ambitious theories and ideas, and looking to engage in long discussions about almost any topic. Despite this intellectual curiosity, reading was particularly difficult for me. I often refused to read and, most likely as a form of self-defense, would go on long rants about the pointlessness of reading. I found a refuge in film and television.

Movies and TV, particularly movies, have always made sense to me. While I could hardly read for more than a minute at a time without losing focus, I found I could watch challenging films that my friends considered boring for hours with total involvement. My intellectual connection with film became so strong that I could not imagine what purpose books could possibly serve.

VARYING SENTENCE STRUCTURE

After writing your draft, review your work for readability. Including sentences that vary in length and structure can enhance the overall quality of the essay and ensure that you are getting your points across in the most effective way possible.

Ironically, after such a tumultuous start to my relationship with the written word, I have grown up to be an avid reader. Still, my affinity for film remains. As I encounter new themes and concepts in other art forms and in my own life, I find that film anchors my intellectual and emotional progress. For me, film has become more than a mere source of entertainment and intellectual stimulation. I have developed relationships with the great films and the great filmmakers that have shaped the way I see the world. I have internalized Hitchcock's fear of imprisonment, Fellini's obsession with the spectacular, and Scorsese's guilt. I have connected with Stanley Kubrick, Woody Allen, and Charlie Chaplin in ways that, although entirely different, in some ways surpass my relationships with some of my closest friends.

While I understand and have been impacted by the language of film, it is not yet a language I can speak. Up to this point, my line of communication through film has been one way—I have been affected by the films of others, but I have not been able to express myself through the medium, at least not beyond my amateur attempts at filmmaking. I aspire to enter into that privileged group of people who can not only experience the films of others but also express themselves through films of their own.

Growing up, my outlet for expression was not an artistic one but rather, a physical one. Tennis was my consuming passion and my commitment to the sport was so complete that I hardly had the opportunity to consider other pursuits in any meaningful way. During my sophomore year of college, a serious injury forced me to take a year and a half away from the sport. Although this was a devastating period for me, I now see my injury as something of a blessing. The absence of tennis in my life left a void that needed to be filled.

It was during this period that my love for film intensified, and I discovered screenwriting as my new outlet for expression. Though the timing of this shift of focus seemed like a mere coincidence at the time, I now realize that my interest in artistic expression could only evolve when my outlet for physical expression receded. My experience with screenwriting has been overwhelmingly positive. I now have the good fortune of seeing life's challenges not just as obstacles that must be overcome, but also inspiration for my work as a writer. I have written constantly, studied screenwriting in class, and read as many books and screenplays as I could in order to improve my craft. Screenwriting has allowed me to channel my creative energies in a way that I had not previously imagined.

Despite its incredibly fulfilling aspects, I have learned that screenwriting is an incomplete medium. The words on the page exist only to be transformed into images on the screen. As fulfilling as screenwriting may be, a screenplay can never really be a vehicle for communication unless it is translated into film. As I result, I hope to gain a deeper understanding of film production in order to fully communicate my stories or the stories of others by using the full power of cinematic expression.

My need to communicate and express myself guides my outlook as an aspiring filmmaker. The two key elements of communication are first having something to say and second having an audience who wants to listen. It seems most contemporary films fall into either the category of films that have something to say that no one wants to watch or films that appeal to a large audience but have nothing to say. The responsibility for modern filmmakers is to walk the tightrope between the two extremes.

If there is one quality of mine that I trust will guide me as an aspiring filmmaker and possibly separate me from my peers, it is a powerful appreciation of the need for films to entertain as well as move their audiences, both emotionally and intellectually. A film that addresses life's most profound issues but does not entertain is no better than a mindless blockbuster that leaves the consciousness of the audience at the moment the credits roll. My dream is to find that rare balance and take part in making films that are entertaining enough to captivate an audience and powerful enough to move them.

WRITER'S WORDS OF WISDOM

I spend basically the entire personal statement describing my interest in film (in my application to film school). It's pretty much taken as a given that you're interested in the subject matter of the graduate degree you're hoping to pursue, so it's not really a good use of the personal statement to just ramble about how you're really, really interested in it. If I were to do it again, I'd definitely focus more on how I hoped to incorporate film work into my interests and experiences that extend beyond just liking movies a lot.

CHAPTER
51

Harvard Graduate School of Education

No classes for an entire year? I could not wrap my head around the idea. Confused not only by the Master's explanation of Oxford University's tutorial system but also by the matriculation gown I most likely sported backwards, I tried to grasp my new reality. So far, this was not what I expected my junior year to be like as a Visiting Student at St. Peter's College in Oxford. Within the first few minutes of arriving at the humbling institution, I was greeted by someone in a squirrel costume and led to my room assignment in a building called Staircase IV.

My tutor handed me a list of lectures I was welcomed to attend but warned that it would be likely that I would not have time to participate in more than a few in a given term. How was it possible that I was to spend the next year with the only obligation of attending two 1-hour tutorials on a weekly basis? I soon found out, and not only did it stretch the limits of my intellectual capacity, but it made me realize the value of education and the many forms that it can take on. With my first assignment of assessing the ramifications of Turkish accession to the European Union, a list of more than 40 resources to consult, and a vague idea of where the Bodleian library was, I spent the next week preparing the claims I would then have to defend in front of my knowledgeable tutor.

While I had been challenged academically at Georgetown, this was the first time I truly had the freedom to learn what I love and to pursue those academic interests with enthusiasm. I can pinpoint this experience as the start to what has taken a few years for me to recognize and develop. My passion is education, I want to be in a position to share that with others, and I know that the Harvard Graduate School of Education would provide me with the foundation I need to embark on this career path.

My ultimate goal is to provide students with that which my own experience in higher education gave me, the opportunity to explore intellectual interests and to identify the implications of these pursuits in a broader context. I can see myself becoming an academic advisor and serving as a resource to students, and I can also see myself delving into higher education policy and working to increase access to higher education for low-income students. And in the more distant future, I envision competing for a Fulbright scholarship to exchange insights on field of higher education with people from all over the world. While I am open to and excited by the number of possibilities a career in higher education offers, I am focused on pursuing the Masters of Education Higher Education Program at the HGSE in order to enrich my understanding of the institutions of higher learning and to become a leader in education.

While it may seem like my role at the FBI's Counterterrorism Division is an unlikely starting point for a career in academic advising, my daily responsibilities involve providing guidance to special agents in the field and ensuring that they have access to the necessary resources to conduct investigations. A given day may include editing an operation proposal from Miami Division, resolving a policy issue with the national security legal team, or preparing a brief to a class of new special agents. That being said, there is no such thing as a typical day, and this is something I would look forward to in a career as an academic advisor. Both my professional and academic careers have required me to become exceedingly resourceful, a quality I anticipate utilizing frequently in counseling students. Although I believe that I have qualities and experiences that will translate to a successful career as an academic advisor, I also know that

PROVIDING CONTEXT TO YOUR APPLICATION

Tell your story the way you want it to be told. The author chooses to focus on how her previous work experience prepared her for her future plans rather than dwelling on the differences in career paths. Make it clear that you have thought through your decision and that what you have done in the past has led you to this moment.

higher education is a very rich and complex field and that the HGSE would allow me to navigate this area of study and enable me to be an effective higher education administrator.

CHAPTER
52

Columbia University
School of International and Public Affairs

What distinct impact do you hope to have on the world in the future? Please be as clear as possible about your future goals, the policy/public service issue(s) you are passionate about, and your personal motivation(s). Be sure to include details regarding the features of SIPA that you believe are integral to helping you in your pursuits and what skills you need to develop to achieve a lasting impact.

A city where policy makers and public officials recognize, understand, and appreciate the economic, political, and scientific connections of today's most urgent environmental issues and in response design smart, innovative, high-impact projects aimed to improve residents' lives, reduce emissions, and increase resilience to climate change. A city where leaders learn from peer cities across the United States and around the world on what projects and policies have worked or failed, and most importantly—why. A city where sustainable objectives are communicated effectively and residents are positively motivated to participate in achieving sustainable goals. A city where residents trust in their public officials to deliver the highest quality public services. As a graduate of the ESP program, it would be my goal to be a public servant who develops and implements policies and programs to make cities like the one described above a reality.

As part of my undergraduate experience, I was fortunate enough to partake in University of Virginia's Semester at Sea study abroad program. During the 4-month educational circumnavigation of the globe, I was exposed firsthand to the interconnected nature of environmental issues. For instance, I learned and subsequently witnessed how decisions regarding natural resource management of the Mekong Delta in Vietnam affected the economic well-being of the communities living on the Delta who were dependent on the natural resource for their livelihood. Another eye-opening example was how a poorly designed public transportation system in the city of El Salvador, Brazil, sequestered poorer populations in favelas, cutting them off from economic opportunities in the city and further exacerbating social inequality. The exposure to global environmental issues I gained from this voyage sparked my interest so fervently that upon my return, I changed my undergraduate study course from focusing solely on international affairs to integrating environmental studies and politics. I believe that SIPA's MPA in Environmental Science and Policy would be the perfect program to build off these studies and acquire new skills to become an effective and well-rounded environmental leader.

I have been fortunate enough to have professional experiences working at organizations that are dedicated to solving some of these issues. For example, the World Resource Institute's (WRI) strategy is to spur progress toward solutions to urgent environmental challenges by providing practical strategies for change and effective tools to implement them. It is my responsibility as Program Coordinator for the Government Sector to communicate to national and international government donors how WRI's programs are effectively making positive change in the world toward achieving environmental and sustainable goals. However, I am no longer satisfied playing a supporting role. The curriculum offered by the MPA ESP will build and enhance my current knowledge and provide practical new skills to become a well-rounded problem solver. The core curriculum's emphasis on science and management analytic tools will build off my United States Agency for International Development (USAID) program management experiences, which includes financial, contract, and project management. The natural science component will enhance and deepen my understanding of Earth systems and how humans interact with these systems. The quantitative and policy analysis courses will provide invaluable opportunities to analyze environmental problems in structured and holistic ways. The social science courses will further deepen my comprehension of the political and economic issues so integrally connected to the causes and effects of environmental problems.

Through my experiences, both educational and professional, I am confident that I am an ideal candidate for this program. I believe the unique skill set offered by the MPA ESP program will provide the perfect professional degree to advance my career in the direction of solving environmental sustainability issues. I pursue this degree in hopes of becoming a professional well-equipped to work with city, state, and federal government to achieve the realization of sustainable, forward-thinking, and healthy cities and communities.

EXHIBITING CONFIDENCE

The author not only conveys how she is interested in obtaining the degree to further her career but she also clearly displays the qualifications and experiences that make her a strong candidate for the program.

CHAPTER 53

New York University
Steinhardt School of Culture, Education, and Human Development

As I walked down the bustling rue Vavin, amongst the cheerful students hurrying into the Luxembourg gardens for lunch, businessmen laughing in the corner café, and beautiful French mothers pushing strollers, I felt, strangely, a sense of belonging. When I first moved to Paris I lived in a limbo—neither a tourist nor a local. After 4 months, however, I had assimilated into society by mastering the French language. I looked and, more importantly, sounded the part of a true Parisian! At last I was at home.

Speaking, reading, writing—these have always come naturally to me. A loquacious 2-year-old, I loved to start conversations with passers-by from my stroller. By age 7, I was searching the dictionary for obscure vocabulary to use during the family dinner conversation. When I was 8, my father taught German to my siblings and me using MUZZY videos, and I fell in love with foreign languages. In high school, I took every French class available, and by college, I knew I wanted to pursue this interest further. Though I excelled with language, I was always aware that communication did not come easily to everyone; my uncle and brother have both worked with speech therapists for autism spectrum and articulation disorder treatment, respectively. Growing up, I wasn't fully aware of the severity of my uncle's autism and wondered why he would revert to snappy one-liners during conversation and why he didn't know that certain behaviors were inappropriate. Now, I am so proud that after years of treatment with behavioral specialists and speech therapists, he is able to live and work independently. My brother saw a speech therapist to fix an articulation disorder when he was 3, and after a few months he was able to speak with perfect clarity. I was proud of my brother as well and impressed that therapy was so effective. The exposure to speech and language therapy within my own family is one of the reasons why I decided to explore this field.

Living abroad was a pivotal point in my life, determining my path toward a career in communication disorders. Becoming fluent in French made me want to explore my own language as well—its linguistic rules, acquisition process, and psychological and social implications. It also strengthened my desire to help others develop and refine their speech and language skills, whether native or foreign. I am applying to graduate school now so that I may fulfill my aspiration to become a speech-language pathologist.

At Georgetown University, I gained a solid academic base that will be invaluable to my graduate studies and future professional endeavors. I also worked all 4 years of college while succeeding with a heavy course load, demonstrating my ability to multitask and take on responsibility, a necessary quality for students balancing clinical hours with graduate studies. The common thread between all of my jobs was working directly with others—giving tours of Congress,

WRITER'S WORDS OF WISDOM

Many SLP schools do not interview prospective students during the application process, so it was important to highlight why I would be a good addition to their school. What exactly will you bring to the table that differentiates you from other students? Your academic, vocational, and volunteer experiences may highlight some qualities you value in yourself. I chose to demonstrate these qualities through a personal example.

teaching English to French students, planning vacations, translating documents for West African immigrants, even working in client services at an e-discovery start-up. On one occasion, an Ivoirian woman began to cry as I transcribed her affidavit for asylum in the United States. I initially thought that remembering her family's murder and her heroic escape had upset her, but I realized that instead she was crying because she had hope and a chance at a new life. I was so moved by her amazing story and glad that I could have helped her in even a small way. One of the traits I value most in myself is that I use my sensitive nature constructively, especially in one-on-one settings. As a speech-language pathologist, I hope to use the patience and perspective I have gained through past experiences to help others in a life-changing way. This career, though challenging, would be so rewarding each and every day. Although I would be joining your program with a different academic background than many students, my unique experiences and genuine interest will be an important asset to the speech community.

WRITER'S WORDS OF WISDOM

I think the above paragraph was especially important to my application because I was applying to a program for which I had not previously studied. I chose to draw upon some professional experiences that related to speech pathology, but you could also talk about a favorite class or club that relates.

In researching potential graduate programs, it became immediately clear that New York University is my ideal choice for its superior academic and clinical resources. When I visited in November, my decision was further justified by the refreshing enthusiasm of the faculty, clinicians, and students I encountered. Academically, I am most interested in learning about speech and language disorders in young children: how phonological, grammatical, and lexical systems develop, and, more importantly, how this knowledge can help those for which communication does not come naturally. The abundant electives in childhood disorders would allow me to specialize in my main area of interest, but I also know that at NYU I would receive a broad-based, comprehensive education and exposure to subjects I have not thought of before. Your unique, interdisciplinary approach between communication disorders, nutrition, vocals, and

SELECTING THEMES FOR THE ESSAY FRAMEWORK

The author crafts a very convincing essay, leaving readers assured that the author has identified the ideal program for her to meet her goals and has the skills required for her pursuits. The author does a masterful job of picking out key experiences from her childhood through her academic life that ultimately guided her to this profession. This essay demonstrates that it does not necessarily matter if your undergraduate background does not match your graduate school goals—choose experiences from your life that highlight why you would excel within your chosen field.

other related fields, would be so valuable for future professional experiences and is another reason why I believe NYU is a fit for me. The size of this program is perfect because it is small enough that students uphold high academic standards and the community is collaborative, yet large enough to attract distinguished faculty and innovative research, manage a successful in-house clinic, and be an esteemed name in the speech community. The clinical opportunities available at NYU through the Speech-Language-Hearing Clinic, the broad network of schools and hospitals available for off-campus practicum and the diverse clientele New York is home to would provide the well-rounded, practical education I am seeking. Furthermore, I want to study in New York because it has been my home for the past couple of years, it is where my support and friends are and it is a city of boundless opportunities.

After becoming a licensed speech-language pathologist, I would like to work with children, particularly those who are developmentally disabled, to treat motor speech and language disorders. I fully believe that NYU has the best means to help me achieve this goal. I am so fortunate to have found a career that combines my linguistic and scientific interests with my aspiration to work with children and help others. The truth is, I simply cannot imagine myself doing anything else.

CHAPTER

54

University of Michigan

Gerald R. Ford School of Public Policy

A few months ago I was consulting with a small business owner named Mary who owned a handmade stationery shop in Ohio. She was struggling because her clients were increasingly migrating to more convenient, online options for similar products, and she was only just beginning to establish an online presence. In our conversations, I gave her a number of recommendations on how to compete by making her website more visible to people searching for her products. I spent considerably more time with her than I usually did, and while I tried to maintain professional distance, I could not help but truly empathize with her plight. She had spent her whole life building a business, perfecting her craft, only to have the market shift right before her eyes. What made her competitive before—quality products and a local consumer base—is no longer sufficient in the face of online consumerism, and she felt completely displaced. I have found too many small business owners who feel the same way.

SHOWING RATHER THAN TELLING

Using an example from the professional setting can be an excellent way to showcase skills and a dedication to learning.

In my last 2 years at Google, I have worked on a close-knit team dedicated to engaging with small businesses. Our goal has been to educate as many businesses as possible about how Google's online tools can help them. Over the phone, over video chat, or by traveling directly to them, I have spent thousands of hours with hundreds of businesses, each with unique goals, needs, and struggles. Every time I work with someone and a lightbulb goes off, or I get a thank-you note specifying how much his or her business has improved, I know I've made a difference. I didn't know that I could have that kind of impact, especially because before starting at Google, I knew very little about online advertising and the small business landscape in this country. I approached my new role like a sponge: I absorbed every piece of knowledge I could about Google's advertising products, the company's mission, and the unique constraints that small businesses face. The more I learned, the more passionate I became about my work.

That raised an interesting question as I started thinking about what to do next. If I am so passionate about my job, why should I do anything else? Why not stay at Google forever? It was in my conversation with Mary this summer that I found my answer. The reason I felt so strongly about my job, and the reason I worked so hard, was because I sensed an injustice. Mary had worked hard her whole life, and at a point when she should have been preparing for retirement, she was worrying about staying in business. So many of the advertisers I worked with were new to using a computer, let alone complicated technical programs like Google's advertising products. Each day they faced an uphill battle to stay current, to stay competitive in their once familiar corner of the market.

CONVEYING PASSION

Passion and drive ooze out of this essay and allow for a clear transition to answering the questions of why grad school, why Michigan specifically, and why now.

Yet it was not only in small business advertising where I sensed deep and disturbing unfairness. What about seniors without adequate medical coverage? Or students who receive abysmal education, teachers who are paid far less than they deserve, or individuals who were barred from equal rights because of who they happen to love? As the daughter of a lifelong teacher and a fiery labor lawyer, it is passion that drives me, and I am happy to say that it always will. Too many fixable inequalities exist in this country; too many serious injustices at every level. I could say in this essay that there is one cause that I plan to champion upon graduating from the University of Michigan, but truthfully, that would be a bold lie. There are a variety of issues I am eager to explore, and the Gerald R. Ford School of Public Policy will challenge me to analyze, discuss, and dissect each of them. Professors and even students will encourage me to refine my positions, support my arguments, and temper my passion with healthy, multifaceted debate. I will work every day to rise to the occasion.

In his inaugural speech, John F. Kennedy made his historic call to action that has energized two generations of citizens to embrace public service, myself included. However, months earlier in a speech accepting the Democratic nomination, he also said, "I believe in a government which acts, which exercises its full powers and its full responsibilities. Government is an art and a precious obligation; and when it has a job to do, I believe it should do it." I feel called to public service because I believe there is more that our country can do for its citizens. We can do better to support the disadvantaged, to fund our school systems, to embrace individuality and diversity, and to plan for a future untarnished by partisan bickering, and the divisiveness to which we are all now accustomed. It may be through more conversations with wonderful people like Mary, but in whatever shape my future unfolds, I will be a part of the dialogue and I will make a difference. I hope that an education at the University of Michigan is my next step on that journey.

WRITER'S WORDS OF WISDOM

Don't overthink your essays. Clear your head, sit down, and write from the heart.

CONCLUSION

Starting the Writing Process

The hard part is over. You have decided that you want to further your education, and you are taking the first steps in making it happen. The authors of the essays provided had very different backgrounds with even more disparate future goals, but all agreed on the same thing. When it comes to the graduate school application process, the most challenging aspect was deciding to apply in the first place, whether it was years in the making or the result of evolving interests. For many, sitting down and writing the admissions essay(s) was the next major hurdle. It may seem funny that providing a 2-page essay could seem so daunting to individuals who spent their undergraduate years writing 20-page research papers and presenting dissertations. However, writing about oneself can prove to be a very challenging exercise, as it requires the writer to thoughtfully consider relevant experiences and academic intentions and then present these ideas within an honest and coherent manner. For some, the task was made simpler by having a specific prompt to address, but for most programs, applicants were offered the opportunity to craft essays based on the topic of their choice. Hopefully, the essays provided sparked some ideas for your prospective topic, but here are some additional questions to consider when making that decision.

1. When did you decide that you were interested in applying to graduate school?

2. Which classes were your favorites when you were an undergraduate student? Were there professors in particular who inspired you?

3. What are your long-term career goals? Is graduate school necessary in order to pursue those career aspirations?

4. Can you think of a time when you held a leadership position? Were there challenges you had to overcome? How did you come to a solution to effect change?

5. Are there particular aspects of the graduate program that attract you? The university's faculty? Research opportunities of interest? The location of the university?

6. What experience will you bring to the program? What, specifically, sets you apart from other applicants?

7. Are you interested in making a career change? Was there something about your prior experience that helped you realize your professional skills and interests?

8. Have you traveled somewhere that had an impact on your perspective?

9. Is there someone in your life who inspires you and who has led you to where you are now?

10. Why is now the ideal time in your life to attend graduate school?

Now, go. Write down all of your ideas and get started. Be sure to leave yourself plenty of time to revise or completely start over. After you have your ideas down on paper, you will be able to better visualize what you want your essay to look like. Avoid falling into the trap of waiting for that perfect topic to hit you; instead, allow the writing process to lead you to it. Once you have completed a draft, go back and review the sample essays to be certain that you are hitting all of the points you want to make within your essay. Remember, most admissions essays are between 500 and 800 words—this does not leave much room to express who you are, why you are a great candidate for your intended program, and why you are interested in the degree, so make sure that each paragraph counts.

After you have something down on paper, show someone. It may be a professor, a friend, or a coworker—someone who you trust to give you honest feedback on your work.

In the draft stage, you should ensure that you have tailored your essay to fit the individual programs to which you are applying, if applicable. This is your opportunity to introduce yourself and to convince admissions officers that you belong in next year's class, so this is not the time to be shy or to make mistakes in grammar or spelling. You have undoubtedly worked hard to be where you are. If you are at the essay-drafting stage, you have likely completed the required admissions examinations and your undergraduate coursework (or are close to being finished), and you can look at the essay as the final opportunity to make your application stand out and make your case for your acceptance.

Congratulations on your decision to apply to graduate school. Best of luck to you on the application process and your future studies!

About the Author

Colleen Reding grew up in Mt. Prospect, IL, and became a proud member of Georgetown University's Class of 2010. Colleen gained acceptance to her first-choice program for graduate study at Harvard University and credits her admission with the outstanding examples of admissions essays from her Georgetown classmates.